Disequilibrium and Macroeconomics

Disequilibrium and Macroeconomics

Volker Böhm

Basil Blackwell

First published 1989

Basil Blackwell Ltd
108 Cowley Road, Oxford, OX4 1JF, UK

Basil Blackwell Inc.
432 Park Avenue South, Suite 1503
New York, NY 10016, USA

British Library Cataloguing in Publication Data

Böhm, Volker
  Disequilibrium and macroeconomics
  1. Open economies. Disequilibria. Macroeconomic aspects
  I. Title
330.12′2

  ISBN 0–631–16532–0

Library of Congress Cataloging in Publication Data

Böhm, Volker
    Disequilibrium and macroeconomics.

    Bibliography: p.
    Includes index.
    1. Equilibrium (Economics) 2. Macroeconomics.
  I. Title.
  HB145.B626 1989   339.5   88–32027
  ISBN 0–631–16532–0

Typeset in 11 on 13pt Times
by Vera-Reyes, Inc.
Printed in Great Britain by T. J. Press Ltd, Padstow, Cornwall

Contents

Preface

The manuscript for this book has grown out of my continued research interests and out of my conviction that economic theory should have more to offer than a description of Walrasian long run equilibria. To limit all theorizing to such equilibrium states, as is currently done by many researchers, not only restricts the usefulness of much of the theory, but it also makes it impossible to discuss the essential features and conditions under which the invisible hand may operate successfully. As theorists direct their attention more and more towards dynamic models again, it seemed desirable and challenging to put some of the theoretic developments of the seventies to the test in an appropriately defined dynamic setting.

The challenge was offered to me in the suggestion of Jean-Michel Grandmont that I survey the literature of the theory of allocations under quantity rationing, both its general microeconomic framework and its contribution to macroeconomics. After rereading the literature on the subject, it became clear that it was almost straightforward to present the general features of the theory of allocations at non-Walrasian prices within microeconomic temporary equilibrium analysis. But to take stock of the impact and influence of such a theory on macroeconomic theorizing was more difficult, and the treatment of it left me with a sense of dissatisfaction. Very little of the published material seemed to apply the same kind of rigour to a dynamic macroeconomic theory as in the microeconomic temporary equilibrium analysis. The effect was to search for a consistent structure which could both serve as a general dynamic macroeconomic model and was a good representative for a temporary equilibrium model, for which the microeconomic allocation model at non-Walrasian prices was applicable. Parallel developments in the theory of overlapping generations models describing explicitly the dynamic behaviour convinced me that the same model could be used for my purpose as well.

The result is the monograph presented here, which in its second chapter presents the current state of the art of the general microeconomic theory of allocations under non-Walrasian prices. The remaining chapters attempt to provide a consistent dynamic macroeconomic model in the overlapping generations setting. The material presented is certainly not completely worked out and many important aspects still need to be structured and analysed in detail. However, I find confirmation and assurance in discussions with colleagues and in the current stream of dynamic economic modelling that the non-Walrasian approach in an overlapping generations model may prove to be a useful addition to our understanding of dynamic economics. After all, it is interesting to learn that full price and wage flexibility in many situations will lead the invisible hand astray.

My primary scientific indebtedness is to Costas Azariadis, whose profound remarks and general concern with dynamics convinced me of the usefulness of adopting the overlapping generations approach. Several visits to the University of Pennsylvania and an invitation to CEPREMAP in Paris set the stage for encouraging and fruitful discussions. Tony Atkinson, Andrea Battinelli, Jürgen Eichberger, Rolf Schmachtenberg and Gerd Weinrich read the complete manuscript at various stages and provided numerous useful and critical comments. These helped considerably to clarify and improve the presentation and the formal arguments. I am grateful to all of them. Needless to say, any remaining errors are my own. My special thanks go to Sabine Wolter, who painstakingly typed the different versions of the manuscript, and to my student assistants who prepared the diagrams again and again, attaining near perfection.

Volker Böhm
Mannheim
July 1988

1

Introduction

The development of macroeconomic theory over the past two decades has created a wide array of different theories, concepts and results which have caused widespread dissatisfaction among those who attempt to resolve the important current economic problems of unemployment, inflation and the balance of payments. Advice from theoretical groups amounts to a list of contradictory recommendations as to the role and direction an economic policy should take. The origin of such conflicting policy suggestions consists in a basic underlying disagreement among macroeconomists on the appropriate or 'correct' model describing the current economic environment. To some this constitutes a crisis of economic theory. If the ground rules of scientific research are the accepted standard for the search for an understanding of the complexities of an economic system, this crisis will be resolved through scientific work and not by declaring one of the current combatants as the winner on the basis of some public opinion poll nor by some singular empirical evidence which seems to support a particular point of view.

One of the fundamental issues among current economic researchers already divided orthodox classical economists and Keynes in a debate more than 40 years ago. Whereas classical economists argued on the premise of a stable self-healing price adjustment process, Keynes asserted that the modern economy does not possess effective mechanisms which, unassisted by government policy, eliminate general excess supply of labour and productive capacity. The classical premise of continued market clearing has been reinstated as one of the major building blocks of what has become known as new classical macroeconomics. Its major proponents such as Lucas, Sargent, Wallace and Barro consider unemployment as an equilibrium phenomenon for which other explanations, among them random exogenous disturbances, information restrictions, search and aspects of the theory of labour contracts, serve as a descriptive basis. However, post Keynesians following the seminal contributions by Clower (1965) and Leijonhufvud (1968) attempted to analyse mechanisms and market outcomes when prices do not attain their equilibrium values, describing situations of involuntary unemployment as one of the possible features to prevail in an economy. Both groups criticize the orthodox macroeconomic models on the grounds that the macroeconomic functional relationships do not sufficiently incorporate the underlying structure of rationally behaving individual agents, thus demanding in principle a more explicit microeconomic foundation for any macroeconomic relationship. The major and almost exclusive emphasis of this demand by the proponents of the new classical macroeconomics is on the expectations of prices and policy variables on which individual agents base their behaviour at any moment of time. This culminated in the formulation of the rational expectations hypothesis which has become the second building block of that part of macroeconomics. However, the development which followed the work of Clower and Leijonhufvud took a more general approach to describe expectations in which agents in general may not foresee the future accurately. This clearly presents a more suitable working hypothesis for any short-run analysis in a temporary framework of an ongoing economy. At the same time this approach begs an answer to the important and non-trivial question of how agents adjust their expectations, since, clearly, long-run steady states are conceptually associated with a correct or 'rational' expectations process.

On both counts (i.e. on the issue of market clearing versus non-market clearing and on the issue of expectations), the theory of temporary equilibrium with quantity rationing represents the more general approach incorporating the market clearing situation with correct expectations as a special case. The two basic ingredients to this theory are an extension and generalization of the model of (sequential) temporary equilibrium as originally suggested by Hicks (1946, 1965) to situations of non-market clearing employing the notion of quantity rationing proposed by Drèze (1975), a paper already circulated in 1971. Among the first contributions to this approach one finds Glustoff (1968), Solow and Stiglitz (1968), Barro and Grossman (1971) and Benassy (1973) attempting primarily a description of Keynesian unemployment phenomena as well as indicating the possibility of different disequilibrium situations under non-market clearing conditions. A first complete and systematic account of the full spectrum of alternative non-market clearing situations in a simplified macroeconomic framework was provided by Barro and Grossman (1976), Benassy (1977a) and Malinvaud (1977), treating explicitly the effectiveness of price and wage policies as well as of government demand policy. Parallel to this development in a macroeconomic context, the literature contains a large number of contributions in a general microeconomic framework. Benassy (1975a, b, 1976a) and Grandmont and Laroque (1976a) consider the general existence question in the competitive and monopolistic framework. Others enlarge the conceptual set-up of Drèze to strategic behaviour under quantity rationing in a deterministic and a stochastic framework (Böhm and Lévine, 1979; Gale, 1979; Heller and Starr, 1979; Weinrich, 1984a, c). Efficiency questions of allocations under rationing in a static framework were treated by Böhm and Müller (1977), Hahn (1978), Balasko (1979, 1982) and Drèze and Müller (1980).

In a second phase some contributions have been made to the important and difficult problems of the role of expectations for equilibria with rationing (Hildenbrand and Hildenbrand, 1978; Neary and Stiglitz, 1983) and of the dynamics of equilibria with rationing (Böhm, 1978; Honkapohja and Ito, 1981, 1983). Some results are available for simple models under stochastic rationing (Honkapohja and Ito, 1985; Weinrich, 1985).

The theoretical development of the theory of quantity rationing has not yet reached a state of consolidation. In particular, the literature contains only few contributions treating the dynamic adjustment process of prices and expectations. In this respect some of the early hopes for new results in the theory of the business cycle have not yet been fulfilled. Some difficult and fundamental problems still have to be solved.

The present monograph attempts to give a systematic account of the important ingredients of a theory of allocations under non-market clearing prices in a constructive way, bridging the gaps between the different models with quantity rationing which exist in the literature. Chapter 2 contains a description of the general microeconomic framework for which a certain degree of consolidation has been reached. It supplies a general characterization of rationing mechanisms, a unified approach to the different notions of equilibria under strategic and non-strategic behaviour of agents, and some discussion of the optimality of equilibria with rationing and of monopolistic equilibria. In essence, this chapter provides a survey of the existing literature on the microeconomic equilibrium theory with quantity rationing at non-Walrasian prices. Because of its level of generality the standards and techniques are those of general equilibrium theory. This is in contrast with the mathematically less sophisticated methods used in all subsequent chapters, which treat models of a macroeconomic type.

Chapter 3 presents a version of a simple prototype macroeconomic model in an overlapping generations setting supplying a synthesis for the diverse classical and Keynesian views of unemployment. Section 3.1 develops the standard IS–LM model using the aggregate demand–aggregate supply format. The derivation of an employment function at non-Walrasian prices displays most clearly the fact that the allocation structure of this model is equivalent to the much quoted contribution by Malinvaud (1977), in spite of the fact that the latter model does not contain a bond market. This equivalence of the two models provides the justification to present a prototype model in section 3.2 without a bond market and to discuss in detail its temporary structure.

Unemployment equilibria in an extended version of the prototype model of chapter 3 are discussed in chapter 4. Section 4.1 introduces inventory holding into the prototype model and section 4.2 presents an extension to situations with bonds and/or credit. The analysis concentrates on questions of the effectiveness of government demand and open-market policies in the short run. Some sources for the reversal of the signs of the standard policy multipliers are exhibited. Chapter 5 describes some of the important dynamic properties of the prototype model of chapter 3 where prices and wages adjust according to the law of supply and demand. The compatibility of long-run steady states with agents' expectations and with the notion of the Phillips curve is investigated. Perfect foresight steady states are analysed, describing the influence of inflation on employment and welfare. A result on generic multiplicity of steady states gives some indication for the existence of cyclical behaviour. Finally, some steady state results are reported for the extended prototype model, in particular readdressing the issue of the long-run effectiveness of monetary policy.

2

Non-Walrasian Prices and Quantity Rationing

The general theory of equilibrium in the tradition of Walras as developed over the last 50 years has provided a sufficiently rich framework and a precise axiomatic formulation of a theory of prices and allocations. This has become known as general equilibrium theory with Walrasian prices. Such prices, if they exist for an economy, provide the complete and satisfactory basis for a decentralized and frictionless allocation mechanism. If each agent follows a prescribed rule of maximizing behaviour at the given prices, the mechanism yields feasible and Pareto-optimal allocations. Although the formal model does not explain why equilibrium prices are obtained, it has been a generally accepted interpretation of the competitive nature of the model and an assumption that prices in the economic environment are always sufficiently flexible to adjust to the Walrasian levels. With this general assumption the analysis is exclusively concerned with describing allocations at equilibrium prices. Apart from some exceptions (notably the so-called non-*tâtonnement* literature) general equilibrium theory makes no attempt at characterizing trading when prices are not market clearing. It was only natural then that the systematic theoretical analysis of such situations was described in an economic and institutional setting of some or complete price rigidity. Such inflexibilities are known to exist in reality. They are also a major element in most of Keynesian macroeconomics where rigidities are explicitly written into the models. Most of the theoretical development of the last 15 years which introduces price rigidities explicitly has become known under the term of fixed-price theory. Taken at face value, this new part of general equilibrium theory provides as little (or as much) of a justification for price rigidities as static Walrasian theory provides a justification for the assumption that prices are sufficiently flexible *and* that equilibrium allocations can always be attained. In a temporary equilibrium setting it is well known that market clearing prices may not exist in many cases (Grandmont, 1974). Therefore, if one denies the possibility of instantaneous price adjustments to their market clearing values, because these do not exist or because trade has to take place before prices can be adjusted, then the need to describe trade at arbitrary non-Walrasian prices arises in a natural way. This in no way implies that prices are rigid in a predetermined way for ever. Rather it imposes the two questions of how allocations are determined at given prices *and* how they adjust after a non-market clearing trade occurred.

The so-called fixed-price theory solves primarily the trade problem after prices have been set. Therefore from a modelling point of view it would be more appropriate to characterize the major body of this new literature as an extension of temporary Walrasian theory, i.e. as a theory of allocation under temporarily non-Walrasian prices including the market clearing situation as a special case. Most of this theory, however, should be considered within the competitive paradigm in which the disequilibrium trade provides a market signal for a price adjustment process. Therefore, the question which of the prices are the most likely to be observed in the short run cannot be answered using this theory. Rather the description of the price dynamics for the medium and for the long run are the important issues here. Chapter 5 contains an analysis of the long-run consequences of the competitive price adjustment.

Apart from the major body of this literature which can be placed within the competitive structure, there exist some recent contributions which consider the short-run price determination as an endogenous part of the model and which show that in the short run non-Walrasian allocations and prices arise as equilibrium outcomes. These contributions belong to the framework of models with monopolistic competition. Some of these are mentioned and discussed at the end of this chapter.

For the evaluation of the importance of quantity rationing models for macroeconomic analysis, it is clearly more appropriate to discuss the issues of rationing within a temporary setting rather than in a purely static one. However, the basic principles and characteristics of quantity rationing are equally applicable to both situations and are more clearly described if the intertemporal complexity of an agent's decision is kept to a minimum. Consequently, for most of this chapter intertemporal aspects will be ignored. Moreover, it is sufficient first to describe the concepts and problems in the context of an exchange economy. The introduction of production requires no conceptual alterations.

2.1   The Basic Model

Assume that the economy consists of a set of agents A and that there are $\ell + 1$, $\ell \geq 1$, commodities in the economy indexed $h = 0, 1, \ldots, \ell$. Each agent $a \in A$ is characterized by a triple $(\tilde{X}_a, \tilde{e}_a, u_a)$ where $\tilde{X}_a = IR_+^{\ell+1}$ is his consumption set, $\tilde{e}_a \in \tilde{X}_a$ his initial endowment, and $u_a : \tilde{X}_a \to IR$ his utility function. Prices p_h, $h = 0, \ldots, \ell$, for all commodities are assumed to be strictly positive with $p_0 = 1$, i.e. commodity zero is chosen as numeraire or 'money'. Trading restrictions will occur on markets $h = 1, \ldots, \ell$, only and all sales and purchases are made against commodity zero. Define $p = (p_1, \ldots, p_\ell) \in IR^\ell$ as the vector of numeraire prices. Then any net trade $x \in IR^\ell$ of agent a at prices $p \in IR_{++}^\ell$ implies a change of his initial endowment of the numeraire equal to $-px$. Therefore, it is convenient to write the set of feasible net trades of agent a as

$$X_a(p) = \{x \in IR^\ell \mid x_h + e_{ah} \geq 0, \ h = 1, \ldots, \ell, \ px \leq e_{a0}\}$$

and the resulting utility as

$$v_a(x) = u_a(e_a + x, e_{a0} - px) \qquad x \in X_a(p)$$

where $e_a \in IR_+^\ell$ with $\tilde{e}_a = (e_{a0}, e_a) \in IR_+^{\ell+1}$.

Let $\xi_a(p) = \{x \in X_a(p) \mid v_a(x) \geq v_a(x'), \text{ all } x' \in X_a(p)\}$ denote the unconstrained or *notional demand* of agent a. Then, a pair $(p^*, (x_a^*)_{a \in A})$ is called a *Walrasian equilibrium* if

(i) $x_a^* \in \xi_a(p^*)$ for all $a \in A$

(ii) $\displaystyle\sum_{a \in A} x_a^* = 0$.

Since Walras's law holds, condition (ii) clearly implies that the excess demand for the numeraire commodity is equal to zero as well. Denote by $P^* \subset IR_{++}^\ell$ the set of Walrasian equilibrium prices.

2.2   Rationing Mechanisms

The basic starting point of non-Walrasian allocation theory is the simple but fundamental observation that utility maximizing net trades of all agents cannot be feasible if a non-Walrasian price $p \notin P^*$ is the only signal given to all agents. Therefore agents must observe or perceive that they cannot realize their notional demands and they will adjust their behaviour accordingly. This in turn implies that they may express net trades on each market different from the notional ones *and* that they may realize transactions different from their expressed net trades. It is useful conceptually to separate each agent's perception of the non-Walrasian situation and its influence on his own trading possibilities into two parts. Given that prices are not market clearing, an agent observes some disequilibrium market signals in addition to prices. These may be aggregate measures of disequilibrium like the unemployment rate, individual restrictions on his own purchases or sales, or other statistics which derive from the situation in the markets. Formally, it is assumed that the signal s_a observed by agent a is given by a vector $s_a \in \mathbb{R}^{k_a}$, where k_a is some finite number. Let

$$s = (s_a)_{a \in A} \in \prod_{a \in A} \mathbb{R}^{k_a} = \mathbb{R}^k$$

denote the vector of signals received by all agents a $\in$ A. The second part of an agent's perception of the non-Walrasian situation describes how he may influence his own trade by expressing different demands, i.e. which rationing scheme is actually used to distribute the shortages across agents on each market. Such schemes are well known from some real markets. Typical candidates are queues, ranking orders or proportional rationing. They may be either deterministic or stochastic. It is clear from this discussion that it is agents' demands that primarily determine the market signals. However, all agents decide on their demands given the market signal and their perception of the rationing scheme. The interaction of these two elements then determines the associated equilibrium configurations. The conceptual separation of these two elements as well as its formal structure used below was suggested by Weinrich (1984a, c).

Assume that the set of agents A is finite and define $Z = \mathbb{R}^{\ell \cdot |A|}$ as the net trade space of the economy. Then, a function

$F: Z \rightarrow S \subset \mathbb{R}^k$ which associates with any demand vector $z \in Z$ the signal $s = F(z)$ is called a *signalling function*. Assume that there is a basic underlying probability space $(\Omega, \mathcal{F}, P)$ which describes all stochastic influences of the rationing mechanism. Then, a *rationing scheme* is a list of functions $(\varphi_a)_{a \in A}$, $\varphi_a: \mathbb{R}^\ell \times S \times \Omega \rightarrow \mathbb{R}^\ell$, $a \in A$, where each φ_a assigns to any demand–signal–event triple (z_a, s, ω) the final transaction $x_a = \varphi_a(z_a, s, \omega)$ of agent a. Finally, the consistency of the rationing scheme and the signalling function defines a rationing mechanism.

Definition 2.1

A list $[(\varphi_a)_{a \in A}, F]$ is called a rationing mechanism if

$$\sum_{a \in A} \varphi_a[z_a, F(z), \omega] = 0 \qquad \begin{matrix} \text{all } z \in Z \\ \\ P - \text{a.e.} \end{matrix}$$

The rationing mechanism is *deterministic* if there exists $\omega_0 \in \Omega$ such that $P(\{\omega_0\}) = 1$ or if φ_a is independent of ω. Otherwise it is *stochastic*.

The general definition of a rationing mechanism allows for a large number of situations. Most of the empirically observed mechanisms can be written in the form of Definition 2.1 whenever expressed demands are transformed into feasible trades. Apart from the technical assumption of continuity, two basic principles are applied to describe the relevant class of rationing mechanisms for a market economy. The first stipulates that voluntary trading prevails in all situations, i.e. no agent should be forced to trade more than he declares that he is willing to trade. The second principle attempts to capture an efficiency property on each market such that binding constraints should not occur if there is additional willingness to trade on both sides of the market.

Assumption R1: Voluntary Trading

A rationing scheme $(\varphi_a)_{a \in A}$ fulfils voluntary trading if

$$|\varphi_{ah}(z_a, s, \omega)| \leq |z_{ah}| \quad \text{and} \quad \varphi_{ah}(z_a, s, \omega) z_{ah} \geq 0$$

holds for all $a \in A$, $h = 1, \ldots, \ell$, $z_a \in \mathbb{R}^\ell$, $s \in S$ and P – a.e.

Assumption R1 states that no agent is forced to trade more or on the other side of the market than he declares. An immediate consequence of the property of voluntary trading is that any rationing function φ_a can be written as

$$\varphi_{ah}(z_a,s,\omega) = \min \left\{ \max \left\{ z_{ah}, \underline{\varphi}_{ah}(z_a,s,\omega) \right\}, \overline{\varphi}_{ah}(z_a,s,\omega) \right\}.$$

Here $\overline{\varphi}_a = (\overline{\varphi}_{a1}, \ldots, \overline{\varphi}_{a\ell})$ and $\underline{\varphi}_a = (\underline{\varphi}_{a1}, \ldots, \underline{\varphi}_{a\ell})$ are functions determining upper and lower bounds of trade on each market $h = 1, \ldots, \ell$ with $\underline{\varphi}_a : \mathbb{R}^\ell \times S \times \Omega \to \mathbb{R}^\ell$ and $\overline{\varphi}_a : \mathbb{R}^\ell \times S \times \Omega \to \mathbb{R}^\ell_+$. For example, one could write $\overline{\varphi}_{ah} = |\varphi_{ah}|$ and $\underline{\varphi}_{ah} = -|\varphi_{ah}|$. The two functions capture the idea of how much an agent can influence his maximum transaction through his own expressed net trade. This leads to the following definition.

Definition 2.2

A rationing function φ_a satisfying R1 is called *non-manipulable* if $(\underline{\varphi}_a, \overline{\varphi}_a)$ are of the form

$$\underline{\varphi}_a(z_a,s,\omega) \equiv \underline{\Psi}_a(s,\omega)$$

$$\overline{\varphi}_a(z_a,s,\omega) \equiv \overline{\Psi}_a(s,\omega).$$

Otherwise, a rationing function is called *manipulable*.

Non-manipulability means that an agent's demand has no influence on his maximum possible transactions. Manipulable and non-manipulable rationing functions each have clear advantages and disadvantages. If a function is manipulable then the strategic behaviour of an agent may lead to excessive overbidding as long as his transaction does not coincide with his notional demand. In the deterministic framework this will certainly result in unbounded demand without any meaningful notion of a binding quantity constraint. Thus, equilibria with respect to a manipulable rationing function may not exist. As will be seen below, however, this weakness of manipulable rationing functions disappears if the mechanism is stochastic. Moreover, manipulability may be required if other conditions for the rationing function are imposed. Conversely, non-manipulable rationing functions may not provide any disequilibrium information. Since an agent's realization does not exceed the upper or lower bound given by the functions $(\underline{\varphi}_a, \bar{\varphi}_a)$, he may have no incentive to express a desired net trade outside the interval $(\underline{\varphi}_a, \bar{\varphi}_a)$, thus not signalling any dissatisfaction with his realized trade. In this case, his expressed demand would coincide with his transaction, yielding the misleading implication that the expressed demands correspond to voluntary (i.e. notional) demands. An example from the labour market illustrates this point quite well. An unemployed agent may not signal his willingness to work because of the non-manipulability of the mechanism. Thus his unemployment may be characterized as voluntary rather than as involuntary.

Let $E\varphi_{ah}(z_a, s) = \int \varphi_{ah}(z_a, s, \omega) P \, d\omega$ denote the expected value of agent a's transaction on market h. The efficiency principle alluded to before then yields the second fundamental property of a rationing mechanism.

Assumption R2: No Short-side Rationing

A rationing mechanism $[(\varphi_a)_{a \in A}, F]$ has no short-side rationing if

$$z_{ah}\left(\sum_{b \in A} z_{bh} \right) \leq 0 \text{ implies } E\varphi_{ah}[z_a, F(z)] = z_{ah}$$

for all $a \in A$, $z \in \mathbb{R}^{\ell \cdot |A|}$ and $h = 1, \ldots, \ell$.

Assumption R2 requires that an agent's expected transaction is equal to his demand if he is on the short side of the market, i.e. if the sign of his demand is different from the sign of the aggregate excess demand. Taken together with R1 this yields that an agent on the short side can realize his demand almost surely. Thus, only agents on the long side of each market will be rationed. In other words R1 and R2 imply that there are no mutually feasible supplies and demands remaining in the market.

In general, rationing mechanisms may involve quite complicated feedbacks across different markets. However, very little is known about such effects in reality, and no convincing theoretical model has been presented using rationing mechanisms which operate across markets. Hence, the assumption of independence across markets will be used here as in most of the literature. For $z \in \mathbb{R}^{\ell \cdot |A|}$ and $h = 1, \ldots, \ell$, let $z_h \in \mathbb{R}^{|A|}$ denote the list of demands $(z_{ah})_{a \in A}$ in market h, and define $S_h \subset \mathbb{R}^{k_h}$ as the non-empty set of possible signals referring to market h.

Assumption R3: Independence across Markets

The rationing mechanism is called independent across markets if

(i) $S = \prod\limits_{h=1}^{\ell} S_h$

(ii) $F = (F_1, \ldots, F_\ell)$ such that
$$F_h : \mathbb{R}^{|A|} \to S_h \qquad h = 1, \ldots, \ell$$

(iii) $\varphi_a(z_a, s, \omega) = (\varphi_{a1}(z_{a1}, s_1, \omega), \ldots, \varphi_{a\ell}(z_{a\ell}, s_\ell, \omega)) \qquad a \in A$

(iv) $\{\varphi_{ah}(z_{ah}, s_h, \cdot)\}_{h=1}^{\ell}$ is stochastically independent.

R3 stipulates that all signalling and rationing is market specific. Finally, in some applications a uniformity or equal treatment property is imposed. In the demand context here this essentially implies that identical demands by different agents should not assign different expected transactions to these agents. In other words, the mechanism should not discriminate according to agents' names or other exogenous criteria.

Assumption R4: Anonymity

The rationing mechanism is called anonymous if for any $s \in S$ and two agents a and a', and for z_a and $z_{a'}$ in $\mathbb{R}^\ell$, $z_a = z_{a'}$ implies $E\varphi_a(z_a, s) = E\varphi_{a'}(z_{a'}, s)$.

It should be observed that all deterministic queuing mechanisms do not fulfil anonymity whereas, if the queuing is random, R4 will hold in most cases. Finally, as a technical requirement it will be assumed that the mechanism is continuous in an appropriate way. Define the distribution of agent a's transactions as

$$\mathcal{D}\varphi_a(z_a, s) = P \circ \varphi_a^{-1}(z_a, s, \cdot)$$

Assumption R5: Continuity

For all $a \in A$ and $(z_a, s) \in \mathbb{R}^\ell \times S$, the distribution $\mathcal{D}\varphi_a$ is continuous in (z_a, s) with respect to the topology of weak convergence.

If the mechanism is deterministic, then R5 implies that the rationing functions φ_a are continuous for all a $\in$ A.

Some examples may serve to illustrate the importance of the assumptions and will help to develop further insight into their implications. For the remainder of this section independence across markets R3 will be assumed.

Example 2.1

This mechanism assigns a uniform upper and lower bound on net trades on every market $h = 1, \ldots, \ell$ as the signal for each agent. Let $z_{ah}^+ = \max\{z_{ah}, 0\}$ and $z_{ah}^- = \min\{z_{ah}, 0\}$ and define for $h = 1, \ldots, \ell$ and any given $z \in \mathrm{IR}^{|A|}$

$$\bar{s}_h = \sup\left\{s \in \mathrm{IR}_+ \mid \sum_{a \in A} \min\{z_{ah}^+, s\} \leq - \sum_{a \in A} z_{ah}^-\right\}$$

and

$$\underline{s}_h = \inf\left\{s \in \mathrm{IR}_- \mid - \sum_{a \in A} \max\{z_{ah}^-, s\} \leq \sum_{a \in A} z_{ah}^+\right\}.$$

Then the signalling function $F: \mathrm{IR}^{\ell \cdot |A|} \rightarrow \overline{\mathrm{IR}}^k$ is defined by $F(z) = (\underline{s}_1, \bar{s}_1, \ldots, \underline{s}_\ell, \bar{s}_\ell)$ with $k = 2\ell$ and $\overline{\mathrm{IR}} = \mathrm{IR} \cup \{-\infty\} \cup \{+\infty\}$. The formal extension of the signalling space from IR^k to $\overline{\mathrm{IR}}^k$ becomes necessary since in the definition above $\bar{s}_h$ may attain $+\infty$ or $\underline{s}_h$ may attain $-\infty$. This occurs on both sides of the market if demands balance or on the short side only. The rationing functions φ_{ah}, a $\in$ A, $h = 1, \ldots, \ell$ are given by

$$\varphi_{ah}(z_{ah}, s) = \max\{\underline{s}_h, \min\{z_{ah}, \bar{s}_h\}\}.$$

The mechanism $[(\varphi_a)_{a \in A}, F]$ is deterministic and non-manipulable and it satisfies all the properties R1–R5.

Example 2.2

The deterministic uniform proportional rationing mechanism on each market separately is the best known among the manipulable ones. Let $Z_h^+ = \Sigma_{a \in A} z_{ah}^+$ and $Z_h^- = \Sigma_{a \in A} z_{ah}^-$. Then the mechanism $[(\varphi_a)_{a \in A}, F]$ is defined by

$$F(z) = (Z_1^+, Z_1^-, \ldots, Z_\ell^+, Z_\ell^-)$$

and

$$\varphi_{ah}(z_{ah},Z_h^+,Z_h^-) = \begin{cases} z_{ah} \min\{- Z_h^-/Z_{h.}^+, 1\} & \text{if } z_{ah} \geq 0 \\ z_{ah} \min\{- Z_h^+/Z_h^-, 1\} & \text{if } z_{ah} \leq 0 \end{cases}$$

for all $a \in A$ and $h = 1, \ldots, \ell$. Clearly, the proportional mechanism fulfils voluntary trading (R1), no short-side rationing (R2) and anonymity (R4). Moreover, it is of a particularly simple form where each agent's trade is a function of his own demand and of aggregate demand and supply only. Mechanisms with the latter properties have a natural appeal for macroeconomic applications and they seem to appear quite frequently if the number of agents is large. Green (1980) discusses an example of random queuing which exhibits these properties. However, he also observed that the class of allowable rationing functions may be quite small if voluntary trading and no short-side rationing are imposed even in a weaker form than that given by R1 and R2. Weinrich (1984c) later established that the uniform proportional mechanism is essentially the only one in that class. To present his result the subscript h for the particular market will be suppressed, so that $z_a \in \mathbb{R}$ and $z \in \mathbb{R}^{|A|}$. Assume that the rationing functions $(\varphi_a)_{a \in A}$ of the stochastic mechanism are of the form $\varphi_a : \mathbb{R}^3 \times \Omega \to \mathbb{R}$ where agent a's trade is the random variable $\varphi_a(z_a,Z^+,Z^-,\cdot)$.

Theorem 2.1 (Weinrich)

Let $|A| \geq 4$ and assume that for every $a \in A$ and $z \in \mathbb{R}^{|A|}$

(R̃0) $\sum_{a \in A} E\varphi_a(z_a,Z^+,Z^-) = 0$

(R̃1) $|E\varphi_a(z_a,Z^+,Z^-)| \leq |z_a|$ and $z_a E\varphi_a(z_a,Z^+,Z^-)| \geq 0$

(R̃5) $E\varphi_a(z_a,Z^+,Z^-)$ is continuous in z.

Then there exist continuous functions $\alpha^+ : \mathbb{R}_+ \times \mathbb{R}_- \to [0,1]$ and $\alpha^- : \mathbb{R}_+ \times \mathbb{R}_- \to [0,1]$ such that for all $a \in A$ and for all $z \in \mathbb{R}^{|A|}$

$$E\varphi_a(z_a,Z^+,Z^-) = \begin{cases} z_a\alpha^+(Z^+,Z^-) \min\{- Z^-/Z^+, 1\} & \text{if } z_a \geq 0 \\ z_a\alpha^-(Z^+,Z^-) \min\{- Z^+/Z^-, 1\} & \text{if } z_a \leq 0 \end{cases}$$

If, in addition, for every $a \in A$ and $z \in \mathbb{R}^{|A|}$

(R̃2) $z_a \sum_{b \in A} z_b \leq 0 \Rightarrow E\varphi_a(z_a,Z^+,Z^-) = z_a$

holds, then $\alpha^+(Z^+,Z^-) = \alpha^-(Z^+,Z^-) = 1$.

It should be noted that all assumptions involve the expected value functions of the rationing mechanism only, i.e. market clearing, voluntary trading and no short-side rationing are required to hold in expectations only. This is substantially weaker than imposing these conditions with probability one. The first part of the theorem states that the (weak) voluntary trading condition and continuity imply a particular linear form of the expectation function of each agent's transaction in his own demand. This means especially that the mechanism is anonymous and manipulable. If the assumption of no short-side rationing is added, then the mechanism must be the uniform proportional one. For the deterministic case the result indicates the striking difference from the non-manipulable mechanism given in example 2.1. There the upper and lower bounds cannot be written as functions of aggregates only. Hence, if non-manipulable rationing mechanisms are used where only aggregates matter, most probably voluntary trading will be violated or there will be rationing on the short side, i.e. forced trading or market inefficiencies will arise.

2.3   Equilibria with Quantity Rationing

Given the rationing mechanism, an agent's demand decision can now be defined in a straightforward way. Recall that the probability distribution of agent a's transactions $\mathcal{D}\varphi_a$ depends on his own demand and the market signal s which he observes, i.e. $\mathcal{D}\varphi_a(z_a,s) = P \circ \varphi_a^{-1}(z_a,s,\cdot)$. Feasibility of transactions with probability one then defines the correspondence of feasible demands for agent a as

$$\beta_a(s) = \{ z_a \in \mathrm{IR}^\ell \,|\, \mathrm{supp}\; \mathcal{D}\varphi_a(z_a,s) \subseteq X_a(p) \}$$

where supp v denotes the support of the measure v. Restricting demands to $\beta_a(s)$ implies in particular that an agent will not be bankrupt with probability one. Given that preferences over transactions are characterized by the von Neumann–Morgenstern utility function v_a, agent a chooses his optimal demand so as to maximize expected utility such that all possible transactions x_a of his demand z_a are feasible. The solution of

$$\max_{z_a} \int v_a(x_a)\mathcal{D}\varphi_a(z_a,s)\; \mathrm{d}x_a = \max_{z_a} \int_\Omega v_a[\,\varphi_a(z_a,s,\omega)]P\; d\omega$$

such that $z_a \in \beta_a(s)$ defines a's effective demand $\zeta_a(s)$. This concept of effective demand seems to be the only acceptable one from a modelling point of view. It uses the standard choice theoretic basis of optimal behaviour given the constraints and the information of an agent. In contrast with the Walrasian theory it distinguishes systematically between demands and transactions. The concept of equilibrium given in the next definition requires that demands and signals correspond with each other, i.e. that all agents observe the correct signal and have no incentive to deviate from their own effective demand.

Definition 2.3

An equilibrium with quantity rationing for the mechanism $[(\varphi_a)_{a \in A}, F]$ is a pair $(z,s) \in \mathrm{IR}^{\ell|A|} \times S$ such that

(i) $z_a \in \zeta_a(s)$ for all $a \in A$

(ii) $s = F(z)$.

This concept of equilibrium was proposed first by Gale (1979) and subsequently used by Weinrich (1984a, b, d). Both researchers work explicitly in the framework of stochastic mechanisms. Most of the earlier work, however (most notably the contributions by Benassy (1975b), Drèze (1975), Böhm and Lévine (1979) and Heller and Starr (1979)), uses deterministic rationing schemes and defines different notions of equilibria under rationing. All these are special cases of the definition above and they will be characterized below. Before describing them, some general remarks can be made. Condition (i) states a best response property of each agent given the market signal. Thus, agent a does not know (or does not exploit) the influence of his own demand on the market signal. Therefore, agent a's demand is not necessarily a best response to all other agents' demands. Hence, an equilibrium does not in general possess the Nash property. This clearly depends on the signalling function F, but also on other features of the economy. Two situations, where the Nash property holds in equilibrium, can be singled out directly. The first is the case of a large economy where each agent's influence on the signal is negligible. The formal description of this situation is provided by an economy with an atomless measure space of economic agents and a signalling function in the form of an integral. This case is treated explicitly by Gale (1979) and Weinrich (1984b) with stochastic rationing. In the deterministic case with finitely many agents, the Nash property holds if the signalling function is the identity map, i.e. each agent knows all other agents' demands and maximizes given that information and the mechanism. This approach was taken by Böhm and Lévine (1979) and by Heller and Starr (1979).

The question whether equilibria with quantity rationing exist at arbitrary non-Walrasian prices raises essentially two issues. Under voluntary trading (assumption R1), the zero demand vector of all agents is always an equilibrium. This is a trivial equilibrium in the sense that it reveals no economic disequilibrium or equilibrium information. It may very well be the outcome of a pessimistic view of each agent regarding the impossibility of a non-zero transaction, leading him to express unwillingness to trade. Different versions of this phenomenon are part of the Keynesian macroeconomic paradigm. Non-trivial equilibria, however, at non-Walrasian prices imply that not all demands can be fulfilled and transactions must be different from the Walrasian ones for some agents. This must mean for them that increasing the demand does not increase expected transactions. Therefore a deterministic rationing mechanism must be non-manipulable at equilibrium if prices are not Walrasian. In the stochastic case, the mechanism must assign positive probabilities to higher transactions under excessively large demands, thus bounding equilibrium demands because of the possibility of bankruptcy. From this rather brief discussion and from the available existence theorems in the literature, it follows that manipulable rationing mechanisms should be stochastic if existence of equilibria is required. In the deterministic case, existence requires non-manipulable mechanisms of some form. To conclude the discussion on existence of equilibria, it should be noted that the failure of existence is not as crucial an issue as in the Walrasian case. If the mechanism fulfils some mild additional assumption, then feasible transactions (without bankruptcy) can be described even if agents receive a wrong market signal. Hence, a non-constant sequence of effective demands and associated market signals may arise which captures very well the true disequilibrium situation and thus indicates the need for price adjustments.

Drèze Equilibria

The remaining part of this section will deal exclusively with deterministic rationing mechanisms. The most widely used and accepted equilibrium concept in the literature in microeconomic models as well as in macroeconomic applications under non-Walrasian prices was suggested and defined by Drèze (1975). His original formulation is in the context of a pure exchange economy, but it was soon applied to temporary equilibrium models (e.g. by Grandmont and Laroque, 1976a). In the macroeconomic context Drèze allocations appear in almost all contributions (see, for example, Malinvaud, 1977 or Barro and Grossman, 1976).

Drèze does not specify a rationing mechanism explicitly but defines signals $s = (s_a)_{a \in A}$ which consist of upper and lower bounds on trades for each agent, i.e. $s_a = (\underline{s}_{a1}, \overline{s}_{a1}, \ldots, \underline{s}_{a\ell}, \overline{s}_{a\ell})$. Each agent perceives that these constraints are exogenously given to him and that he is allowed to express only demands which respect these constraints. Let

$$\beta_a^D(s_a) = \{z_a \in X_a(p) \mid \underline{s}_{ah} \leq z_{ah} \leq \overline{s}_{ah}, h = 1, \ldots, \ell\}$$

denote the set of Drèze-feasible net trades. Then the set of Drèze demands $\zeta_a^D(s_a)$ is defined by

$$\zeta_a^D(s_a) = \{z_a \in \beta_a^D(s_a) \mid v_a(z_a) \geq v_a(z_a') \text{ for all } z_a' \in \beta_a^D(s_a)\}.$$

Definition 2.4

A list of demands $z = (z_a)_{a \in A}$ and a list of constraints $s = (s_a)_{a \in A}$ such that $s_a = (\underline{s}_{a1}, \overline{s}_{a1}, \ldots, \underline{s}_{a\ell}, \overline{s}_{a\ell})$ for all $a \in A$ is an equilibrium in the sense of Drèze (a D-equilibrium for short) if

(i) $z_a \in \zeta_a^D(s_a)$ for all $a \in A$ and $\Sigma_{a \in A} z_a = 0$
(ii) for all $h = 1, \ldots, \ell$,

$$z_{ah} = \underline{s}_{ah} \text{ for some } a \in A \text{ implies } z_{bh} < \overline{s}_{bh} \text{ for all } b \in A$$

$$z_{ah} = \overline{s}_{ah} \text{ for some } a \in A \text{ implies } z_{bh} > \underline{s}_{bh} \text{ for all } b \in A.$$

Condition (i) imposes individual utility maximizing demands which balance in the aggregate. This implies that each agent's transaction is equal to his demand. In other words the list of demands in a D-equilibrium is itself a feasible allocation and *not* a set of demand and supply signals from which a mechanism has to determine a feasible allocation. As a consequence no agent signals to the market that he would like to trade more. In the case of unemployment, for example, an unemployed worker does not reveal that he would like to work. Hence, neither aggregate nor individual demands would indicate that a situation with rationing prevails. Thus, the Drèze demands alone do not yield adequate measures of a disequilibrium situation.

Condition (ii) imposes that binding constraints occur at most on one side of a market. This so-called one-sidedness property leaves supply (demand) unrationed if demand (supply) is facing binding constraints. This property excludes the existence of any further mutually feasible and desirable trade in each market between any two agents, one from the rationed and one from the non-rationed side. In this sense, the condition implies a certain type of market efficiency at the given constraints and demands. It is related to the no short-side rationing assumption for mechanisms. The following two propositions establish the relationship between the D-equilibrium and the equilibria with quantity rationing.

Proposition 2.1

Every D-equilibrium is an equilibrium with quantity rationing with respect to the non-manipulable rationing mechanism

$$\varphi_{ah}(z_{ah}, s_{ah}) = \min \left\{ \max \left\{ z_{ah}, \underline{s}_{ah} \right\}, \overline{s}_{ah} \right\}$$

for all $a \in A$, $h = 1, \ldots, \ell$ and some F with $s = F(z)$.

The result follows directly from the fact that $\zeta_a^D(s_a) \subset \zeta_a(s)$ for all $a \in A$. For the converse relationship, i.e. whether an equilibrium with quantity rationing yields an allocation which is a D-equilibrium, some additional requirements have to be fulfilled. It is straightforward to see that the condition of no short-side rationing (R2) does not imply the one-sidedness property imposed by Drèze. In fact, at an equilibrium with quantity rationing a mechanism may be extremely inefficient with binding constraints on both sides of a market, making it impossible to fulfil the one-sidedness condition by Drèze. Moreover, if demands balance in equilibrium, most mechanisms fail to reveal in which direction non-binding quantity constraints may be chosen to fulfil the one-sidedness condition. These two observations motivate the additional assumptions which are needed to demonstrate that the allocation of an equilibrium with quantity rationing corresponds to a D-equilibrium.

Proposition 2.2

(Let $(\tilde{z},\tilde{s})$ denote an equilibrium for the rationing mechanism $[(\varphi_a)_{a\in A},F]$ and assume that $\Sigma_{a\in A}\tilde{z}_{ah} \neq 0$ for all $h = 1, \ldots, \ell$. If R1, R2, R3 and R5 hold and if for all $h = 1, \ldots, \ell$

$$\sum_{b\in A} \tilde{z}_{bh} < 0 \text{ implies } \sup_{z'_{ah}} \varphi_{ah}[z'_{ah},F(\tilde{z})] > \tilde{z}_{ah} \text{ for all } a \in A$$

R6

$$\sum_{b\in A} \tilde{z}_{bh} > 0 \text{ implies } \inf_{z'_{ah}} \varphi_{ah}[z'_{ah},F(\tilde{z})] < \tilde{z}_{ah} \text{ for all } a \in A$$

are satisfied, then the pair $[(x_a),(s_a)]_{a\in A}$ is a D-equilibrium where, for all $a \in A$, $x_a = \varphi_a[\tilde{z}_a,F(\tilde{z})]$ and $s_a = (\underline{s}_{a1},\overline{s}_{a1}, \ldots, \underline{s}_{a\ell},\overline{s}_{a\ell})$ is defined by

$$\underline{s}_{ah} = \inf_{z_{ah}} \varphi_{ah}[z_{ah},F(\tilde{z})]$$
$$\overline{s}_{ah} = \sup_{z_{ah}} \varphi_{ah}[z_{ah},F(\tilde{z})].$$

The proof will be sketched very briefly. R1 and R2, i.e. voluntary trade and no short-side rationing, imply that for all agents on the short side of the market trade equals demand which by R6 is less in absolute value than the maximal possible transaction:

$$\sum_{b\in A} \tilde{z}_{bh} < 0 \text{ and } \tilde{z}_{ah} \geq 0 \text{ implies } x_{ah} = \tilde{z}_{ah} < \overline{s}_{ah}$$

$$\sum_{b\in A} \tilde{z}_{bh} > 0 \text{ and } \tilde{z}_{ah} \leq 0 \text{ implies } \underline{s}_{ah} < x_{ah} = \tilde{z}_{ah}.$$

Hence, $[(x_a),s_a]_{a\in A}$ fulfils the one-sidedness condition. Continuity R5 then yields $x_a = \varphi_a[\tilde{z}_a,F(\tilde{z})] \in \zeta_a^D(s_a)$ for all $a \in A$. The following example serves to illustrate that the additional assumption R6 is not in conflict with some of the earlier ones. In fact, it belongs to the class of non-manipulable mechanisms where the signalling function is modelled after the uniform proportional rationing function. The example satisfies the assumptions R1–R4, R6 and continuity R5 except at zero.

Example 2.3

Suppressing the index for each market, $[(\varphi_a)_{a\in A},F]$ is defined by

$$\varphi_a(z_a, s) = \max\left\{\underline{s}_a, \min\{z_a, \overline{s}_a\}\right\}$$

and

$$\overline{s}_a = \left\{z_a \cdot g\left(-\frac{Z^-}{Z^+}\right) \middle| z_a \geq 0\right\}$$

$$\underline{s}_a = \left\{z_a \cdot g\left(-\frac{Z^+}{Z^-}\right) \middle| z_a \leq 0\right\}$$

where $g:\mathbb{R}_+ \to \mathbb{R}_+$ is any continuous function with $g(x) = x$ if $x \leq 1$ and $g(x) > x$ if $x > 1$.

The two propositions 2.1 and 2.2 provide the basis for considering the concept of Drèze allocations as a natural extension of the competitive allocation theory to describe non-Walrasian allocations in deterministic models. The allocations can be generated as outcomes of equilibria with quantity rationing where market signals and consistent choice theoretic behaviour are compatible with each other. In fact, given the information, each agent exploits all his strategic possibilities. The one-sidedness condition eliminates inefficiencies of trade in each market and it captures quite naturally the disequilibrium features of Keynesian economics. This will be demonstrated in detail in chapter 3.

Since the definition of a D-equilibrium does not specify how the quantity constraints are distributed among agents, in general there exist multiple equilibria or even a continuum for the same vector of non-Walrasian prices. To remedy such an indeterminacy, additional assumptions on the distribution of the quantity constraints have to be imposed, such as, for example, uniformity of the constraints (as was done by Drèze in his original paper) or proportionality. A different route to more specific results is to generate Drèze allocations through rationing mechanisms following proposition 2.2. A third possibility consists of selecting Drèze allocations according to other exogenous criteria, like Pareto optimality, maximal levels of transactions on particular markets, rationing on the same side on all markets, or minimizing the number of markets with binding constraints. Some of these approaches lead to unique equilibria. In spite of these possibilities, the general disadvantage of Drèze allocations remains. Since demands and transactions are not distinguished, the allocation reveals no genuine disequilibrium information which describes agents' dissatisfaction about the allocation and which could be used as a basis for a theory of price adjustment. One possibility of how market signals can be constructed for D-equilibria is described in section 5.4.

Nash Equilibria

The discussion at the beginning of this section, of whether the Nash property holds at equilibria with quantity rationing, indicated already that it holds for specific signalling functions. The special case where the signal of each agent consists of the full vector of all other agents' demands was suggested independently by Heller and Starr (1979) and by Böhm and Lévine (1979).

Let $[(\varphi_a)_{a \in A}, F]$ denote a rationing mechanism such that $F(z) = z$ and define for each $a \in A$ the vector of effective demands of all agents other than a by $z_{\hat{a}} = (z_b)_{b \in A, b \neq a}$. Then the rationing function φ_a as perceived by agent a can be written as $\varphi_a(z_a, s) \equiv \widetilde{\varphi}_a(z_a, z_{\hat{a}})$ for all $z \in \mathbb{R}^{\ell \cdot |A|}$. Since each agent observes the vector of effective demands of all other agents, his maximization in formulating his own effective demand implies that it is best against the demands of all other agents. Hence, definition 2.3 yields that an equilibrium with quantity rationing has the Nash property, i.e.

(i) $z_a^* \in \zeta_a(s^*)$ for all $a \in A$

(ii) $s^* = F(z^*) = z^*$

implies for all $a \in A$

$$v_a[\varphi_a(z_a^*, s^*)] = v_a[\widetilde{\varphi}_a(z_a^*, z_{\hat{a}}^*)]$$
$$\geq v_a[\widetilde{\varphi}_a(z_a, z_{\hat{a}}^*)] \qquad \text{for all } z_a \in \mathbb{R}^{\ell}.$$

Since the assumption that $F(z) = z$ defines a special case of a rationing mechanism, it is not surprising that propositions 2.1 and 2.2 have appropriate analogues establishing the relationship between Nash equilibria and Drèze allocations (see Böhm and Lévine, 1979). Without giving a formal statement, these results say (a) that every Drèze allocation can be generated by an equilibrium with quantity rationing with the Nash property for some non-manipulable rationing mechanism, and (b) that equilibria with quantity rationing which possess the Nash property yield Drèze allocations provided that the assumptions of proposition 2.2 are fulfilled. These results indicate an additional justification in support of Drèze allocations.

K-Equilibria

An alternative approach to effective demand and to fix-price equilibria was provided by Benassy (1975b, 1976b). Here the presentation in Benassy (1982b), which provides the most direct comparison with the general concept of an equilibrium with quantity rationing introduced above, will be followed. In essence Benassy uses non-manipulable rationing functions but introduces a different concept of effective demands.

Benassy develops his framework from a list of market by market rationing functions ψ_{ah}, $a \in A$, $h = 1, \ldots, \ell$, where $x_{ah} = \psi_{ah}(z_h)$ determines agent a's transactions if $z_h = (z_{ah})_{a \in A}$ is the vector of demands in market h. The functions ψ_{ah} satisfy market clearing, i.e. $\Sigma_{a \in A} \psi_{ah} = 0$ for every h, voluntary trading R1 and no short-side rationing R2. In order to model an agent's perception of his trading constraints, Benassy defines signalling functions $(\underline{F}_{ah}, \overline{F}_{ah})$ determining lower and upper bounds $(\underline{s}_{ah}, \overline{s}_{ah})$ for each agent on every market by

$$\underline{s}_{ah} = \underline{F}_{ah}(z_{\hat{a}h}) = \min \left\{ \psi_{ah}(z_{ah}, z_{\hat{a}h}) \middle| z_{ah} \in \mathbb{R} \right\}$$
$$\overline{s}_{ah} = \overline{F}_{ah}(z_{\hat{a}h}) = \max \left\{ \psi_{ah}(z_{ah}, z_{\hat{a}h}) \middle| z_{ah} \in \mathbb{R} \right\}.$$

Each agent believes that the mechanism is the non-manipulable one given any pair of trading constraints, i.e.

$$x_{ah} = \varphi_{ah}(z_{ah}, \underline{s}_{ah}, \overline{s}_{ah}) = \min \left\{ \overline{s}_{ah}, \max\{z_{ah}, \underline{s}_{ah}\} \right\}.$$

Hence, the list $(\varphi_{ah}, \underline{F}_{ah}, \overline{F}_{ah})$, $a \in A$, $h = 1, \ldots, \ell$, defines a rationing mechanism with the particular feature that agent a's signals are independent of his own demands.

Given a quantity signal $s_a = (\underline{s}_{ah}, \overline{s}_{ah})_{h=1}^{\ell}$, Benassy rightly observes that the utility maximizing demand $\zeta_a(s_a)$ will typically be multivalued. This follows immediately since a binding constraint on some market implies that any larger demand on this market will be optimal as well. In order to avoid the multiplicity of $\zeta_a(s_a)$, Benassy defines a unique effective demand for each market taking into account only the constraints on all other markets. Combining these ℓ different demand quantities into a vector yields the Benassy effective demand vector $\zeta_a^B(s_a)$. Formally, assume that v_a is strictly quasi-concave and, for each $h = 1, \ldots, \ell$, let $\zeta_{ah}^B(s_a)$ denote the unique component h of

$$\arg \max \left\{ v_a(x_a) \middle| x_a \in X_a(p), \underline{s}_{ak} \leq x_{ak} \leq \overline{s}_{ak}, k \neq h \right\}.$$

Then $\zeta_a^B(s_a) = (\zeta_{a1}^B(s_a), \ldots, \zeta_{a\ell}^B(s_a))$ defines the Benassy effective demand. This notion of effective demand is based on the so called dual-decision hypothesis suggested by Clower (1965). It attempts to capture the idea that binding constraints on some markets lead to a revision of demands in other markets, which implies spillover effects across markets. In general, these effective demands are different from the binding constraints and thus different from transactions, so that they may serve as indicators of disequilibrium on each market. In particular, it follows from the construction that for each market separately the effective demand reveals that the constraint is binding if and only if the demand exceeds the given constraint. However, the procedure of maximizing market by market is completely arbitrary and displays some conceptual weaknesses which cannot be compatible in general with overall maximization taking the realization into account. In general, the resulting transactions may lead to inconsistencies. It was pointed out by Grandmont (1977a) that the resulting transaction may not be in the budget set, i.e. $\varphi_a[\zeta_a^B(s_a), s_a] \notin X_a(p)$, or it may not be optimal given the constraints. However, strict quasi-concavity of the utility function avoids these two difficulties (Benassy, 1982b, propositions 7.1 and 7.2).

Proposition 2.3

Assume that v_a is strictly quasi-concave. Then

(i) $\zeta_a^B(s_a) \subseteq \zeta_a(s_a)$

(ii) $\varphi_a\left[\zeta_a^B(s_a), s_a \right] \in \zeta_a^D(s_a)$.

A K-equilibrium as suggested by Benassy is now defined as a list of effective demands which produces consistent signals and feasible transactions.

Definition 2.5

A list $(z_a, s_a, x_a)_{a \in A}$ of demands, signals and trades is a K-equilibrium if

(i) $z_a = \zeta_a^B(s_a)$ all $a \in A$

(ii) $\dfrac{\underline{s}_{ah} = \underline{F}_{ah}(z_{\hat{a}h})}{\overline{s}_{ah} = \overline{F}_{ah}(z_{\hat{a}h})}$ all $a \in A$, all $h = 1, \ldots \ell$

(iii) $x_a = \psi_a(z)$ all a ∈ A.

It follows immediately from the construction of the signalling functions and from proposition 2.3 that each K-equilibrium is an equilibrium with quantity rationing with respect to a non-manipulable rationing mechanism, and that the transactions are optimal given the constraints provided that the utility functions of all agents are strictly quasi-concave. Moreover, since the signalling functions of each agent are assumed to be independent of his own demand, a K-equilibrium possesses the Nash property. Finally, under the same proviso as above, K-equilibria yield Drèze allocations if the rationing mechanism satisfies no short-side rationing. This result, which does not require additional assumptions concerning the rationing mechanism as in proposition 2.2, can be demonstrated directly using the property of revealing binding constraints (Benassy, 1982b).

Proposition 2.4

The allocation of any K-equilibrium corresponds to a D-equilibrium if all utility functions are strictly quasi-concave and if the rationing mechanism satisfies R2.

To conclude the description of K-equilibria and their properties, it should be noted that in general the zero demand vector of all agents is not an equilibrium. The concept of effective demand generates non-zero trade offers even under the most severe quantity constraints if trade is desirable. Hence, trivial equilibria do not occur. In connection with proposition 2.4 this implies that K-equilibria yield a non-trivial selection from the set of D-equilibria. The selection does depend, however, on the particular rationing mechanism.

2.4 Efficiency of Equilibria with Quantity Rationing

Relative to the set of first best Pareto-optimal allocations there are essentially two sources of inefficiencies for allocations at non-Walrasian prices. One source is the non-Walrasian price itself. Although there exist situations where an equilibrium at a non-Walrasian price yields a first best Pareto-optimal allocation, this is the exception rather than the rule. The second source of inefficiency arises out of the choice of the particular allocation rule at the non-Walrasian prices at which the value of net trades is equal to zero for all agents. The inefficiencies clearly depend on the choice of the rationing mechanism. However, as will be shown below, the very nature of an equilibrium with quantity rationing implies some inefficiencies in general which cannot be overcome, unless some redistributive scheme in addition to the rationing mechanism is adopted. In the following analysis we consider the efficiency properties of Drèze allocations.

The point of reference for the analysis of the efficiency of Drèze allocations is the set of Pareto-optimal allocations under the restriction that each agent trades on the budget set, given the non-Walrasian price p. More precisely, let $BCPE(p)$ denote the set of budget-constrained Pareto-optimal allocations. A feasible allocation x belongs to $BCPE(p)$ if and only if there exists no other feasible allocation x' such that, for all agents a $\in$ A, $x'_a(p) \in X_a(p)$ and

$$u_a(e_a + x'_a, e_{0a} - px'_a) \geqslant u_a(e_a + x_a, e_{0a} - px_a)$$

with at least one strict inequality. The following example and discussion is taken from Böhm and Müller (1977). Figure 2.1 describes the situation in net trade space for an economy with $\ell = 2$ and two agents labelled a and b. x^*_a and x^*_b are the notional demands of the two agents. The utility functions of the two agents are such that their respective level sets are concentric circles around x^*_a and x^*_b. Therefore, the set of budget-constrained Pareto-optimal allocations BCPE consists of the line $[x^*_a, -x^*_b]$. It is straightforward to see that $x_a = x_b = 0$ is the only Drèze allocation with a zero demand rationing level on both markets. (x^*_a, x^*_b) is also the unique K-equilibrium with the same Drèze allocation. It is obvious that the point zero is not efficient and therefore the set of Drèze allocations is not a subset of BCPE in general. The reason for this phenomenon is that the behaviour of agents which respects quantity constraints market by market does not reveal the existence of mutually preferable trades which involve simultaneous exchanges on several markets. Thus, the one-sidedness condition on every market, which guarantees market by market efficiency, prevents that mutually preferable exchanges are carried out across markets. This feature clearly corresponds to an equivalent phenomenon in a macroeconomic

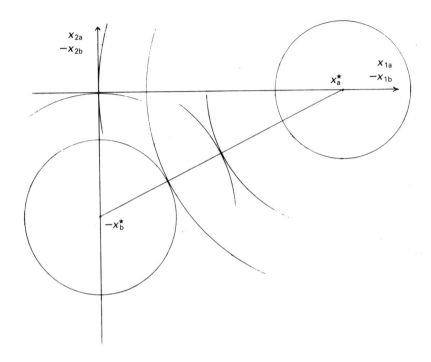

Figure 2.1

setting. Unemployment may be due to insufficient commodity demand which in turn is low because of insufficient income of consumers. A simultaneous increase in employment and production may result in a preferred allocation.

The result above is clearly not due to the choice of a poorly performing rationing mechanism. Hence, measures to improve the allocation have to use some form of forced trade or they employ specific transaction possibilities across markets without rationing. The latter approach is taken by the concept of the so-called coupon equilibrium, a concept proposed by Hahn (1978) and discussed in detail by Drèze and Müller (1980) and Balasko (1982). A coupon price system $q \in \mathbb{R}^\ell$ determines exchange ratios at which agents may trade in addition to the market prices $p \in \mathbb{R}^\ell_{++}$. Thus the coupon prices are specifically designed to enable agents to trade across markets to overcome the inefficiencies of one-sided quantity constraints. Formally, a coupon equilibrium for a given non-Walrasian price p consists of a feasi-

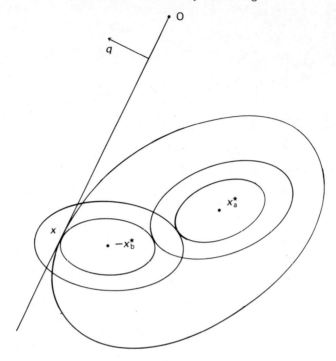

Figure 2.2

ble allocation x and a coupon price $q \in \mathbb{R}^{\ell} \backslash \{0\}$ such that, for all $a \in A$, the net trade x_a is maximal in $X_a(p)$ with the additional restriction that $qx_a = 0$. Such equilibria generate allocations which improve Drèze allocations in general. However, there are situations where a coupon equilibrium does not generate a budget-constrained Pareto-optimal allocation. Figure 2.2 taken from Balasko (1979) characterizes such a situation for an economy with two agents a and b and $\ell = 2$. As before x_a^* and x_b^* denote the notional demands and x is the unique coupon equilibrium. In the example the initial endowment distribution is wrong in a certain sense, which may be overcome by introducing transfers in coupons (for a discussion of these issues and results see Drèze and Müller, 1980).

The preceding paragraphs discuss the efficiency issue at given non-Walrasian prices. Since these prices cause a departure from overall Pareto optimality in the first place, it is an important issue whether a change in prices may lead to another equilibrium with quantity rationing which is Pareto better. The ultimate question

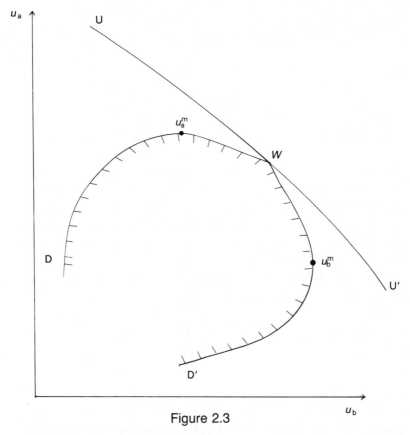

Figure 2.3

would be whether changing a non-Walrasian price p to a Walrasian price p^* generates necessarily a Pareto improvement. In general, the answer is again negative (Böhm, 1984). To see this, consider an economy with two agents a and b and the set of all Drèze allocations. If a or b behave as a fully informed monopolist on the set of Drèze allocations, they can each choose prices and quantity constraints in such a way that they obtain a utility level larger than the ones at any p^*. Thus, for each agent, in general there exists a positive utility gain if he changes a Walrasian price p^* to his own monopoly price. Hence, under standard regularity conditions, changes from prices in the neighbourhood of a monopolistic Drèze allocation to a Walrasian price p^* will decrease the monopolist's utility. Therefore, a change to a Walrasian price and allocation does not yield a Pareto improvement, in general.

Figure 2.3 describes the set of Drèze allocations in utility space relative to the set of all feasible allocations of the economy. The line UU' represents the utility frontier of the economy, W the Walrasian utility allocation, and u_a^m and u_b^m the two monopolistic equilibria. The set inside the curve DD' represents the set of Drèze allocations. It is clear from the diagram that Pareto improvements from either of the monopoly equilibria involve income redistributions between the two agents.

The example indicates that monopolistic behaviour may lead to equilibria with quantity rationing and non-Walrasian prices. Hence, in general, an approach using a notion of monopolistic equilibrium where prices and quantity constraints are determined endogenously would eliminate one of the basic criticisms often raised against non-Walrasian allocation theory, i.e. the need for an explanation of why prices are non-Walrasian in the first place. The pure monopoly case is only one possibility in this direction. Some of the general qualitative properties of this approach along with the existing extensions to economies with production are reported in the next section. The discussion of the contributions treating the case of monopolistic competition in a more macroeconomic set-up are deferred to the end of the next section.

2.5 Monopolistic Equilibria with Quantity Rationing

It has long been accepted as a general premise that monopolistic elements are the major reason for the existence of equilibria at non-Walrasian prices. To use such modelling elements, however, in support of equilibria with quantity rationing raises issues about the relationship of D-equilibria and equilibria with monopolistic competition. As the example indicated, a monopolist may strictly gain by choosing prices and quantity constraints in such a way that the resulting allocation is a D-equilibrium. This means in particular that the allocation can be supported by quantity constraints which respect voluntariness and one-sidedness. Although the pure monopoly situation is very special, only this case will be treated. Its qualitative implications, however, carry over to the situation with several monopolistic agents.

Two questions will be discussed here. The first question addresses the issue whether the possibility of choosing quantity constraints in addition to prices creates an additional gain to the monopolist. In other words, is rationing always strictly beneficial for the monopolist? The second question deals with the more general issue whether the utility maximizing choice of prices by the monopolist against the given competitive offer curve of the rest of the economy yields a D-equilibrium, i.e. whether the monopolist himself behaves as if he were quantity constrained respecting the one-sidedness condition. For the remainder of this section it will be assumed that the utility functions of all agents $a \in A$ are strictly monotonic and strictly quasi-concave, so that notional excess demand is unique for all prices.

Let $b \in A$ denote the monopolist and define as the choice set for the monopolist given the competitive behaviour of all agents other than b the set

$$Z_{A \backslash \{b\}} = \left\{ (p,z) \in \mathbb{R}^{2\ell} \,\big|\, p \gg 0, z = \sum_{a \neq b} \xi_a(p) \right\}.$$

Then the monopolist chooses $(p,z) \in Z_{A \backslash \{b\}}$ which maximizes his utility. Therefore a monopolistic equilibrium belongs to

$$ME_b = \arg \max \left\{ v_b(e_b - z, e_{b0} + pz) \,\big|\, (p,z) \in Z_{A \backslash \{b\}} \right\}.$$

If the monopolist can choose prices as well as quantity constraints for the rest of the economy respecting one-sidedness, his choice set becomes

$$DE_{A \backslash \{b\}} = \Big\{ (p,z) \in \mathbb{R}^{2\ell} \,\big|\, p \gg 0, \text{ there exist } (z_a, s_a) \in \mathbb{R}^{3\ell}, a \neq b$$
such that

(i) $z_a \in \zeta_a^D(p, s_a)$ all $a \neq b$ and $z = \sum_{a \neq b} z_a$

(ii) $\forall h = 1, \ldots \ell$
   $z_{ah} = \underline{s}_{ah}$ for $a \in A \backslash \{b\}$ implies $z_{a'h} < \overline{s}_{a'h}$ for all $a' \in A \backslash \{b\}$
   $z_{ah} = \overline{s}_{ah}$ for $a \in A \backslash \{b\}$ implies $z_{a'h} > \underline{s}_{a'h}$ for all $a' \in A \backslash \{b\}$ $\Big\}$.

Since $DE_{A \backslash \{b\}} \supset Z_{A \backslash \{b\}}$, it follows immediately that

$$\max \left\{ v_b(e_b - z, e_{b0} + pz) \,\big|\, (p,z) \in DE_{A \backslash \{b\}} \right\}$$
$$\geq \max \left\{ v_b(e_b - z, e_{b0} + pz) \,\big|\, (p,z) \in Z_{A \backslash \{b\}} \right\}.$$

Therefore, invoking a D-equilibrium for the rest of the economy, the monopolist cannot lose, and he will gain in general.

Theorem 2.2 (Böhm et al., 1983)

If $\ell = 1$ or $|A \backslash \{b\}| = 1$, then

$$\max\left\{v_b(e_b - z, e_{b0} + pz)\,\middle|\,(p,z) \in Z_{A\backslash\{b\}}\right\}$$
$$= \max\left\{v_b(e_b - z, e_{b0} + pz)\,\middle|\,(p,z) \in DE_{A\backslash\{b\}}\right\}.$$

This result states that the possibility of rationing for the monopolist does not yield an additional gain if there are only two commodities or only one competitive agent. Hence, price control alone is sufficient to exploit all monopoly power. It is intuitively clear that the result extends to an arbitrary number of commodities and competitors if all of them have identical preferences and endowments. However, as an example in the same paper indicates, $\ell \geq 2$ and different competitive agents provide an incentive for the monopolist to use quantity rationing to his benefit in general. In this case the monopolist can exploit the different individual spillover effects from the competitors, thus increasing his own utility. The result of the same paper also implies that for the case of two commodities ($\ell = 1$) and an arbitrary number of competitors, the monopolistic equilibrium is a D-equilibrium, i.e. at the monopolistic equilibrium (p_m, z_m) there exist one-sided quantity constraints s_b for the monopolist such that $-z_m \in \zeta_b^D(p_m, s_b)$. A formal proof of this result is contained in the paper by Schmachtenberg (1987), and a further example with this property for an economy with production, $\ell = 2$ and two consumers is given by Böhm (1984). However, Schmachtenberg shows that for $\ell > 2$ in general a monopolist's choice in ME_b cannot be sustained by quantity constraints s_b and voluntary trading for the monopolist at the monopoly price if aggregate notional excess demand of the competitive part of the economy displays some Giffen goods. Hence, although monopolistic equilibria do explain the existence of non-Walrasian prices, the resulting allocations are not D-equilibria in general if the principle of voluntary trading is applied to the monopolist as well.

The foregoing discussion reveals that equilibria with monopolistic competition do not support equilibria with quantity constraints in general. While the analysis was carried out under the assumption that the monopolist knows the true demand curve of the competitors, other researchers have used the perceived demand approach to define monopolistic equilibria with quantity rationing. These are most notably Benassy (1976a), Grandmont and Laroque (1976a), Negishi (1979) and Hahn (1978). Except for the model due to Hahn these models do not investigate the rationality of the conjectured or perceived demand curves in equilibrium. Two further contributions by Hart (1982) and Silvestre (1986) describe equilibria with quantity rationing and strategic price and wage setting, assuming full knowledge of the true demand curves.

Benassy (1976a, 1982b) combines the elements of monopolistic price setting and of quantity rationing in a way closest to the preceding analysis. Firms are the price-makers. They form their expectations and their perception of demand on the basis of observed quantity constraints and all other prices. They choose their own prices so as to maximize expected profits. Consumers maximize utility given prices and quantity constraints. Then, a list of all prices and quantity constraints is an equilibrium with price-makers according to Benassy if for each firm its prices are best against all others at the given quantity constraints which fulfil the Drèze conditions. Thus, such a monopolistic equilibrium is a D-equilibrium by definition which is consistent with certain demand perceptions of the monopolists.

Benassy's formulation seems to cover a wide range of possible cases. Since it is exogenous to the model which firm controls which prices, i.e. which prices are endogenously determined and which are kept fixed or assumed to be flexible, the two extreme situations of complete monopolistic competition and of completely fixed prices appear as special cases. However, as Benassy points out, there may not exist such equilibria in some cases under standard assumptions. An interesting extension from a macroeconomic point of view includes wage setting by consumers, an idea also presented by Grandmont and Laroque (1976a). In such a context the macroeconomic issue of whether strategic price and wage setting typically leads to non-Walrasian unemployment equilibria becomes important.

Hart (1982) and Silvestre (1986) make an attempt to describe equilibria with quantity rationing and strategic price and wage setting where agents know the true notional and effective demand curves of the whole economy. Both economists present specific examples of a static economy with production where workers set wages and producers (shareholders) set prices. Hart's model contains a continuum of negligible consumers and producers who take prices and wages as given. However, syndicates of workers and producers set wages and prices assuming that their strategic behaviour has no effect on income. In contrast, Silvestre chooses a model akin to the one by Malinvaud with one worker and one producer-shareholder. His major result is that no Nash equilibrium exists, whereas Hart shows, among other things, that a Nash equilibrium does exist for his model and that workers are not fully employed in equilibrium. It seems clear that the divergence of the two results has its origin in the different assumptions on the number of agents. However, it is unlikely that Hart's existence result is robust if the number of agents is finite. In such a case the assumption that strategic wage and price setting has no effects on income is no longer justified. The example by Böhm (1984) of an economy similar to that described by Silvestre also suggests that a Nash equilibrium for the price–wage game does not exist. Both papers imply that this non-existence result does not depend on the particular choices of the technology and of consumer preferences. Therefore, it remains an open question whether a price–wage setting Nash equilibrium generates nontrivial equilibria with quantity rationing which display Keynesian features.

2.6 Summary

The preceding analysis presented the description of the fundamental building blocks of a general theory of allocations at non-Walrasian prices. Starting with the general assumption that all concepts and results should be based firmly in a general model with optimizing agents given their preferences, endowments and a market structure with price-taking behaviour, four main questions were pursued.

1 What are the rules or mechanisms which allocate shortages in a market, since notional demands and supplies do not match under non-Walrasian prices? Which general principles of allocation govern such rules and what influence do they have on the form of the mechanism?

2 What are the consequences of the rationing mechanisms for the behaviour of individual agents and which are the associated equilibrium configurations?

3 Since optimizing agents behave strategically in their demands under the general framework proposed, it is essential to distinguish strictly between the equilibrium configuration and the resulting allocation. Therefore it is important to analyse the

features of such disequilibrium allocations, investigate their properties and scrutinize them with respect to some generally accepted criteria of market allocations.

4 What is the relationship of the disequilibrium allocations proposed, here exclusively the set of allocations in the sense of Drèze, to other non-Walrasian allocations, in particular to monopolistic equilibria?

Investigating question (1) leads to the two fundamental properties of voluntariness and no short-side rationing which have a natural appeal for a market economy and which imply certain qualitative restrictions for the form and structure of mechanisms. These are shown for the deterministic as well as for the stochastic case. They induce specific properties with respect to the phenomenon of manipulation.

The application of rationing mechanisms at non-Walrasian prices to the allocation problem implies that maximizing agents behave strategically given the available signals in the market and their information about the mechanism. Although there exist some clear connections between the literature of mechanism design and implementation and the theory proposed here, these issues are not pursued. Within the framework of market signals and rationing mechanisms an appropriate equilibrium concept follows from this structure. The existence of such equilibria is discussed and they are examined with respect to their Nash property. An important aspect of the strategic demands as measures of disequilibrium, which may serve as indicators for a theory of dynamic price adjustment, is treated.

Two essential properties of disequilibrium allocations describe the set of acceptable outcomes. They were originally proposed by Drèze and correspond to a general principle of market by market efficiency and to the voluntariness assumption for mechanisms. Conditions are provided under which Drèze allocations are generated as equilibrium outcomes of the strategic behaviour of agents, and some optimality properties of such allocations are exhibited. The conceptual generality of the two principles suggested by Drèze makes the associated outcomes clear candidates for any macroeconomic disequilibrium model, since they capture in a straightforward way typical Keynesian features. This supplies the justification for using Drèze allocations in the macroeconomic model which is analysed in the remaining chapters. One proposal

with respect to the rationality discussion of disequilibrium allocations, namely the concept of conjectural equilibria, is not treated
in the text, but some bibliographical notes are contained in
section 2.7.

The relationship of Drèze allocations to monopolistic equilibria
is provided for some specific examples. This is done on the basis
of the general supposition that monopolistic price setting behaviour is one of the major sources of the existence of non-Walrasian
prices. Although the available results are very specific, they seem
to indicate that allocations under monopolistic price setting typically do not fulfil the two Drèze properties.

The available macroeconomic literature contains almost no
contributions which go beyond an application of the notion of
Drèze allocations as describing disequilibrium situations. There
remains a wide array of open problems and questions, e.g. how
strategic behaviour under a given mechanism changes macroeconomic outcomes. For the case of stochastic rationing mechanisms
only one contribution (Weinrich, 1984c) has been made so far.
And the problem of monopolistic behaviour which includes price
and/or wage setting leaves a large open area for further research.

2.7 Bibliographical Notes

1   Grandmont (1977a) attributes the first systematic studies of
quantity rationing in a general equilibrium framework to Glustoff
(1968), Younès (1970a, b, 1972), Drèze (1975) and Benassy
(1973). Drèze treats a more general case with partially flexible
prices between given bounds. The equilibrium concept requires
that binding quantity constraints prevail only in those markets
where price bounds are binding as well.

2   The first contributions with an explicit analysis of rationing
used deterministic schemes. Benassy (1977b) observed the existence problem for deterministic manipulable schemes. Benassy
(1977b), Gale (1979), Green (1980), Svensson (1980) and Weinrich (1984c) treat cases with stochastic rationing.

3   In addition to the two equilibrium concepts of Drèze (1975)
and of Benassy (1973, 1975b), Younès (1970a, 1975) independently suggested a third non-strategic equilibrium concept, which
in most cases coincides with that of Drèze. Silvestre (1982b)

provides a discussion of the conceptual differences as well as an extensive analysis and comparison of all three concepts.

4 Hahn (1977, 1978) introduced the notion of conjectural equilibrium in an attempt to explain why prices do not change in a market when agents observe binding quantity constraints. Such an equilibrium makes the fixed non-Walrasian prices an endogenous outcome of the utility maximizing behaviour of agents. In Hahn's model, however, the endogenous price setting depends on subjectively conjectured trading. Since conjectures by individual agents can be quite arbitrary, there exist many conjectural equilibria. The refinement to so-called rational conjectures may lead to inconsistencies (see Gale, 1978). However, John (1985) shows that under arbitrary conjectures the set of allocations under voluntary trade coincides with the set of conjectural equilibria.

3

Macroeconomic Models with Quantity Rationing

The formal structure presented in chapter 2 supplies a systematic point of departure for the description of disequilibrium phenomena such as unemployment, excess supply and involuntary stock accumulation in commodity markets, which are at the heart of Keynesian macroeconomics. Since situations of partial or full price and wage rigidities appear as the major sources of disequilibrium in macroeconomic models of the Keynesian type, the theory of allocations at non-Walrasian prices seems to lend itself immediately to an application to macroeconomic models as well. In order to apply the techniques and concepts above in a meaningful way, the model of an exchange economy has to be extended to include production as well as elements of a theory of money and other financial assets. This, as is well known, requires a model with a temporary structure in which trade is possible at successive dates and the stores of value for agents carry a positive price. Therefore, in what follows, we shall adopt the framework of temporary equilibrium theory in which money and/or bonds, for example, play an essential role. In all the following we shall not incorporate a richer structure of financial assets or any kind of forward markets.

As to the nature and problems of temporary Walrasian theory there exists a sizeable literature (e.g. Grandmont, 1977a, 1982a, 1983), treating among other things the important and difficult question of existence of temporary equilibria. Although the existence issue will be treated here as well, it is not of primary importance. In particular, the allocation process implied by the theory of quantity rationing at given prices is independent of whether a temporary Walrasian equilibrium exists or whether it is unique. Therefore, the application of the equilibrium concept of the previous chapter to macroeconomic questions will centre around questions of characteristics of allocations and how they depend on prices, wages and policy parameters. Contrary to most of traditional macroeconomic theory the explicit incorporation of all prices in the relevant behavioural equations and the systematic description of all market feasibility conditions under rationing will reveal additional insights as to how prices determine different types of equilibria under quantity constraints. Moreover, it will be shown that the effectiveness of policy measures depends crucially on which particular disequilibrium regime prevails.

3.1   Aggregate Demand and Aggregate Supply – A First Approach

Some economists have used the approach of Barro and Grossman (1976), Benassy (1976b) and Malinvaud (1977) to identify the traditional Keynesian model, in particular its standard IS–LM form, as a special case of a model with quantity rationing (see, for example, Danthine and Peytrignet, 1981, 1984; Benassy, 1983; Sneesens, 1984). One difficulty in a direct application of Malinvaud's model has been the lack of a bond market. It is the purpose of this section to establish that the standard macroeconomic approach using the aggregate demand and supply functions of the Keynesian model leads directly to a description of a macroeconomic model with quantity constraints. Moreover, if price and wage effects are fully incorporated in this model, then its characteristics correspond exactly to a special case of the allocative structure of the model due to Malinvaud (1977) identifying the three typical equilibrium regimes under rationing. The approach presented here combines the standard IS–LM analysis with the methodology suggested by Benassy and Malinvaud (see also Malinvaud, 1982, and Benassy, 1983).

Starting from the accounting identity that nominal national income Y is the sum of total consumption expenditure C and investment expenditure I, assume that total consumption (i.e. private plus government) is a function $C(Y, \alpha)$ where α denotes some vector of government policy parameters like tax rates, government purchases etc. For the moment these need not be specified any further. Investment expenditure is assumed to be a function of the price level p and the interest rate r, homogeneous of degree one in p and decreasing in r. Hence real investment demand can be written as $i(r)$ with $i' < 0$.

Private agents hold wealth in the form of money and of interest-bearing bonds. Taking the standard textbook approach, it will be assumed that the government maintains a fixed total money supply $\bar{M}$ and finances its expenditures through taxes and new bonds. Let $M(Y, r)$ denote the demand function for money with the standard interpretation that money serves as a store of value and for transactions purposes. This implies some form of a Clower constraint (cash in advance restriction) which forces agents to hold non-interest-bearing money as well as bonds. As is well known, this same feature could be obtained without transactions restrictions if the return on bonds were sufficiently random and private agents were risk averse. Then r would have to be interpreted as the expected rate of return on a bond held from one period to the next.

Taking the two market clearing conditions together, one obtains the two equations

$$py - C(py, \alpha) - pi(r) = 0 \tag{3.1}$$

$$M(py, r) - \bar{M} = 0 \tag{3.2}$$

Let $C_Y = \partial C/\partial Y$, $C_\alpha = \partial C/\partial \alpha$, $M_Y = \partial M/\partial Y$ and $M_r = \partial M/\partial_r$ denote the partial derivatives of the consumption function and of the money demand function respectively.

Assumption A1

$$0 < C_Y < 1, \quad C(Y, \alpha)/Y > C_Y, \quad i' < 0,$$
$$M_Y > 0, \quad M_r < 0.$$

A solution of (3.1) and (3.2) for given $(\alpha, \bar{M})$ defines the aggregate demand function $y = D(p, \alpha, \bar{M})$. If assumption A1 holds, differentiating (3.1) and (3.2) yields

$$\frac{\partial D}{\partial p} = -\frac{y}{p} \frac{[C(Y, \alpha)/Y - C_Y] M_r + pi' M_Y}{(1 - C_Y) M_r + pi' M_Y} \tag{3.3}$$

$$> -\frac{y}{p}.$$

Therefore, under assumption A1, the aggregate demand curve will be downward sloping with a slope less in absolute value than y/p. This implies in particular that increasing real demand along D is associated with decreasing money income.

To complete the model the supply side of the economy, i.e. production and the labour market, has to be described. Assume that short-run aggregate real output y can be written as a monotonically increasing function of labour input ℓ, i.e. $y = F(\ell)$. This formulation implies that all other factors like capital, equipment etc. determining output are fixed. Let $w > 0$ denote the wage rate. Maximization of short-run profits with all other capacity costs fixed yields notional labour demand as $h(w/p) = \arg\max [p F(\ell) - w\ell]$ and notional commodity supply as $F[h(w/p)]$. If F is concave in the relevant range, then $h' < 0$ and commodity supply is upward sloping in p and downward sloping in w.

Assume that total labour supply $L > 0$ is exogenously given. Then, applying the one-sidedness condition implies the following definition of an equilibrium with quantity rationing.

Definition 3.1

Given (p, w) and $(\alpha, \bar{M})$, a pair (y, ℓ) is an equilibrium with quantity rationing if

$$y = \min\{D(p, \alpha, \bar{M}), F(\ell)\} \tag{3.4}$$

$$\ell = \min\{\bar{L}, h(w/p), F^{-1}(y)\}. \tag{3.5}$$

Since F is a strictly monotonic function the two conditions can be reduced to a single condition

$$\begin{aligned} y &= \min\{D(p, \alpha, \bar{M}), F[\min\{\bar{L}, h(w/p)\}]\} \\ &= \min\{D(p, \alpha, \bar{M}), F(\bar{L}), F[h(w/p)]\} \end{aligned} \tag{3.6}$$

which determines y and $\ell = F^{-1}(y)$. The function $S(p, w, \bar{L}) = F[\min\{h(w/p), \bar{L}\}]$ defines the amount of output that the production sector is willing to supply taking labour market feasibility into account. Thus, $S(p, w, \bar{L})$ represents the aggregate supply function for arbitrary prices and wages. It is straightforward to identify the two extreme cases of aggregate supply discussed in the macroeconomic literature as special cases. $S(p, w, \bar{L})$ possesses the derivative properties $S_p = \partial S/\partial p > 0$ and $S_w = \partial S/\partial w < 0$ if $\bar{L}$ is not binding and productive capacities are used fully.

Under these assumptions it is easy to see that for every $(p, w) \gg 0$ and $(\alpha, \bar{M})$, (3.6) yields a unique equilibrium with quantity rationing. Figure 3.1 portrays a typical situation in (p, y)-space for a given wage rate w. The graph of the function (3.6) which defines equilibrium output y has been drawn as the thick curve. Given w, from figure 3.1 it is clear that there are three distinct rationing situations depending on prices p and wages w.

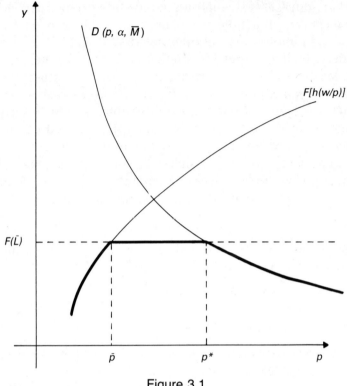

Figure 3.1

Classical unemployment equilibria

For (p, w) such that $p < \bar{p}$, price equals marginal costs, i.e. the marginal product of labour equals the real wage. Moreover, labour is not fully employed since $y < F(\bar{L})$, i.e. $\ell = F^{-1}(y) < \bar{L}$, and $D(p, \alpha, \bar{M}) > y$. Hence, there exists supply rationing on the labour market and demand rationing on the commodity market while the producer realizes his notional supply and demand. This is a situation of classical unemployment.

Keynesian unemployment equilibria

For (p, w) such that $p > p^*$ one has $F(\ell) = y = D(p, \alpha, \bar{M}) < F(\bar{L}) < F[h(w/p)]$. Therefore there exists unemployment with a marginal product of labour larger than the real wage. On the commodity market notional supply is larger than actual output which is equal to aggregate demand. Hence, there exists supply rationing on both markets which defines an equilibrium of Keynesian unemployment.

Repressed inflation equilibria

For (p, w) such that $\bar{p} < p < p^*$, full employment prevails, but notional labour demand is larger than employment and aggregate commodity demand is larger than output. Hence, there exists demand rationing on both markets. This is an equilibrium of repressed inflation.

The complete characterization of all equilibria with quantity rationing can now be obtained by analysing the function (3.6) for all $(p, w) \geqslant 0$. Since output and employment are in a one-to-one relationship, there exists a function $\mathscr{L} : \mathbb{R}^4_{++} \rightarrow \mathbb{R}_+$ associating with each price–wage pair (p, w) and exogenous parameters $(\alpha, \bar{M})$ the actual employment level $\ell = \mathscr{L}(p, w, \alpha, \bar{M})$ given by

$$\mathscr{L}(p, w, \alpha, \bar{M}) = F^{-1}(\min\{D(p, \alpha, \bar{M}), F(\bar{L}), F[h(w/p)]\}$$
$$= \min\{F^{-1}[D(p, \alpha, \bar{M})], \bar{L}, h(w/p)\}. \quad (3.7)$$

$\mathscr{L}$ is well defined and incorporates all the information about which equilibrium with quantity rationing is obtained at which $(p, w, \alpha, \bar{M})$. For given $(\alpha, \bar{M})$ the geometric representation of $\mathscr{L}$, originally suggested by Benassy (1973) and Malinvaud (1977), yields the characterization given in figure 3.2. There, the regions of classical unemployment, of Keynesian unemployment and of repressed inflation are denoted C, K and I respectively. It can easily be deduced from (3.6), or from figure 3.1 and from the fact that aggregate supply is decreasing in w, that there exists a unique Walrasian temporary equilibrium (p^*, w^*). Moreover, the boundaries of the three regions drawn as thick curves are of the particular form indicated. The thin lines represent the level sets of the function $\mathscr{L}$, i.e. the points (p, w) with constant employment, indicating decreasing levels as (p, w) moves away from I and from (p^*, w^*). The boundaries $C \cap I$ and $I \cap K$ can be constructed directly from figure 3.1. For $(p, w) \in C \cap K$, (3.6) implies equality of aggregate demand and aggregate supply, i.e. $D(p, \alpha, \bar{M}) = S(p, w) < F(\bar{L})$. Differentiation yields

$$\left. \frac{dw}{dp} \right|_{C \cap K} = \frac{S_p - D_p}{-S_w} > -\frac{S_p}{S_w} = \frac{w}{p}.$$

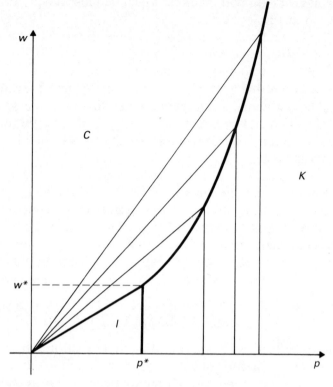

Figure 3.2

Finally, the equilibrium interest rate on the bond market is obtained from (3.2) once output is determined using (3.6).

The function $\mathscr{L}$ determining employment and therefore output yields all comparative statics results in a straightforward way, since it is defined for all values of the policy parameters and all prices and wages. This assumes, of course, that the aggregate demand function is well defined, i.e. that the system (3.1) and (3.2) has a unique solution for all $(p, \alpha, \bar{M})$.

The price and wage effects on employment can be read off directly from figure 3.2 which displays very clearly the differences for different rationing states. Specifically, wage increases have no effect on employment under Keynesian unemployment, while under classical unemployment wage increases will reduce employment. Here the real wage w/p is the relevant variable. In contrast, price increases have opposite effects, increasing employment under classical unemployment but decreasing it under Keynesian unemployment. The effects on total income Y and on the interest rates are also quite different in the two regions C and K. From the inequality given in (3.3) it follows that employment and output increases under Keynesian unemployment caused by price and wage changes imply a decreasing money income, while income increases with employment under classical unemployment. This implies that the effects on the interest rate are also opposite to each other.

Changes in government policy parameters $(\alpha, \bar{M})$ imply changes for the aggregate demand curve, leaving aggregate supply conditions unchanged. This implies immediately that small changes in α or $\bar{M}$ have no employment or interest rate effect for given (p, w) under classical unemployment. Moreover, the full-employment real wage does not change, but the Walrasian price p^* and wage w^* must change in the same proportion. Consider an expansionary policy change which is characterized by an outward shift of the aggregate demand curve (see figure 3.1). It is straightforward to see that this shifts the boundaries $(I \cap K) \cup (C \cap K)$ to the right with the new Walrasian price and wage equal to $\lambda (p^*, w^*)$ for some $\lambda > 1$. Figure 3.3 indicates the change where the dotted line is the boundary $(C \cap K) \cup (I \cap K)$ before the expansionary measure. The isoemployment lines in the Keynesian region change to the right in the appropriate way. Hence, at given $(p, w) \in K$ any (small) expansionary effect increases employment. The associated multipliers can be obtained from (3.6) as

$$\frac{dy}{d\alpha} = \frac{\partial D}{\partial \alpha} \quad \text{and} \quad \frac{dy}{d\bar{M}} = \frac{\partial D}{\partial \bar{M}}.$$

Finally, the two possible policy measures which cause an expansionary effect should be analysed. One such possibility represented by a change in α is an autonomous increase in government purchases or a decrease in taxes. The other possibility would be an expansionary monetary policy. Both measures correspond directly to the equivalent measures usually analysed in the traditional IS–LM framework, implying the same qualitative effect on income and on the interest rate.

To conclude the description of the standard model of aggregate demand and supply, a few remarks concerning the government's budget constraint may be informative. Suppose government policy parameters are a proportional tax rate $0 < \tau < 1$ on total

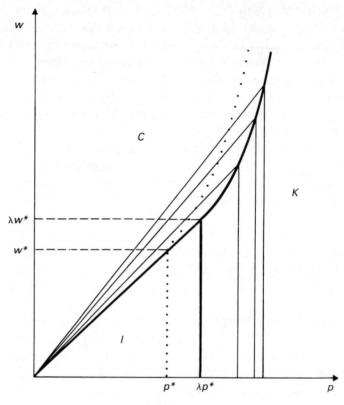

Figure 3.3

income, a quantity $g > 0$ of government purchases of goods. Government debt is issued in the form of one-period bonds sold at their discounted value in one period and redeemed at their nominal value the following period. Let M_t denote the initial money holdings at the beginning of period t and B_t the number of outstanding government bonds at the beginning of period t. If $r > 0$ is the interest rate, then the number B_{t+1} of bonds sold in period t implies public revenue of $B_{t+1}/(1 + r)$ in period t and a volume of public debt of B_{t+1} to be redeemed in period $t+1$. Then the government budget constraint can be written as

$$\Delta M = M_{t+1} - M_t$$
$$= pg - \tau Y_t + B_t - B_{t+1}/(1 + r) \qquad (3.8)$$
$$= p\{g - \tau F[\mathscr{L}(p, w, \tau, g, M_t)]\} + B_t - B_{t+1}/(1 + r).$$

Since y and r are determined endogenously, it is clear that, in general, B_t will be different from B_{t+1} under a constant monetary policy with $\Delta M = 0$. In particular, the model allows no general conclusion whether positive or negative deficits are more probable in any of the three disequilibrium regions. Moreover, the sign and size of the deficit will be constant over time for a sequence of temporary equilibria with rationing if none of the parameters change. Hence, such a sequence will in general be one of constant expansion or contraction of public debt held by private individuals. This seems highly implausible as a description of any optimizing behaviour of households or firms for more than a one-period model. The major reason for this result is that private wealth (money plus bonds) plays no role in determining aggregate demand. Combined with the special form of the demand function for money, this implies a particular form of savings behaviour hardly consistent with intertemporal utility maximization. One of the extensions of the model presented in the next sections will be precisely to incorporate explicitly the intertemporal choices made by consumers. This will imply that, in general, consumption and bond demand cannot be written as functions of aggregate income and of the interest rate alone. In addition, it is shown that the long-run effects of increases in public debt are quite different from the short-run effects usually predicted by the traditional Keynesian model. Moreover, the long-run consequences of the government budget constraint analysed in chapter 5 confirm in principle the results in the literature on dynamic Keynesian models (Blinder and Solow, 1973, 1974); Tobin and Buiter, 1976).

3.2   Prices, Wages and Employment

One of the criticisms raised in the previous section concerning the behavioural assumptions of the consumption sector was that in an intertemporal context asset demand was modelled in a rudimentary way which did not make explicit the optimizing behaviour of individual agents. The important contribution of the theory of quantity rationing in an intertemporal setting consists of the fact that it supplies a consistent choice theoretic microeconomic foundation to a general model, which in its aggregative form allows all questions of a macroeconomic nature to be analysed while including a full description of all allocative issues which are typically treated in microeconomic models only. This important methodological view was most forcefully and completely presented by Benassy (1973), Barro and Grossman (1976) and Malinvaud (1977). Apart from some minor differences in the presentation and the choice of the particular model, all three work with the same basic intertemporal model with the three commodities labour, consumption and money. Consumers make intertemporal consumption choices, while a single profit maximizing firm is using an atemporal neoclassical production function. The government purchases commodities and raises taxes. This section contains a variant of this kind of model which possesses the same qualitative macroeconomic features as those of the economists given above.

The Model

Consider an ongoing economy at a particular time period t. One homogeneous output is produced from one input factor labour. The government purchases a quantity $g > 0$ of the commodity at the market price p_t, and it raises taxes from profits at a proportional tax rate τ, $0 \leqslant \tau \leqslant 1$. Money serves as a unit of account and as a store of value for consumers. Budget deficits or surpluses are the only source for changes of the money stock held by consumers; thus their net asset position changes if and only if the deficit is different from zero. Equivalently, total net savings of consumers are always equal to the deficit.

Consumers and Production

The model contains two groups of consumers, namely worker-consumers who supply labour and consume and shareholder-consumers who do not work, receive net profits and consume. For each group, the overlapping generations structure, which seems to be the natural framework for an ongoing stationary economy, will be chosen. Generations of each group of consumers are identical and of equal size. Each generation lives for two periods. Throughout the section it will be assumed that each generation consists of one consumer of each type.

Shareholders and workers consume in both periods of their lives, but they differ in their source of income during the first period. Workers receive labour income whilst shareholders receive all net profits. Consider first the behaviour of old consumers. Consumption of both types will be financed by savings, i.e. by the accumulation of wealth during the first period of their life in the form of money. Let $M_t > 0$ denote the total stock of money held by old consumers at the beginning of period t. Then, given the current commodity price p_t, aggregate consumption demand of old consumers is given by M_t/p_t.

Let π_t denote current profit income of the young shareholder. For a consumption plan $(x_t, x_{t+1}) \geqslant 0$ let $u^s(x_t, x_{t+1})$ denote his two-period utility function. Assuming that he makes a point forecast $p^e_{t+1} > 0$ for the commodity price in period $t + 1$, his current notional commodity demand x^*_s is given by the solution of

$$\max_{x_t} u^s(x_t, (\pi_t - p_t x_t)/p^e_{t+1}) \qquad \text{such that } \pi_t - p_t x_t \geqslant 0$$

Assumption C1

$u^s : \text{IR}^2_+ \to \text{IR}$ is a twice continuously differentiable, monotonically increasing, strictly concave function such that $\partial^2 u^s/\partial x_t \partial x_{t+1} \geqslant 0$. For any sequence $(x^n_t, x^n_{t+1}) \geqslant 0$ converging to (x_t, x_{t+1}),

(i) $\partial u^s/\partial x_t(x^n_t, x^n_{t+1}) \to +\infty$ \qquad if $x_t = 0$

(ii) $\partial u^s/\partial x_{t+1}(x^n_t, x^n_{t+1}) \to +\infty$ \quad if $x_{t+1} = 0$.

Let $c^s (p_t, p^e_{t+1}, \pi_t) = x^*_s$ denote the notional commodity demand function and $m^s (p_t, p^e_{t+1}, \pi_t) = \pi_t - p_t x^*_s$ the associated demand function for money. Then the properties of these two functions listed in the following lemma can be shown in a straightforward way.

Lemma 3.1

Assumption C1 implies that for all $(p_t, p^e_{t+1}, \pi_t) \geqslant 0$

(i) $c^s (p_t, p^e_{t+1}, \pi_t) > 0$ \qquad and \qquad $m^s(p_t, p^e_{t+1}, \pi_t) > 0$

(ii) c^s and m^s are differentiable and $0 < p_t \, \partial c^s/\partial \pi_t < 1$.

A worker consumes in both periods but supplies labour only when young up to some maximal amount $\bar{L} > 0$. Assume that his preferences are separable over consumption and labour and that they are represented by a utility function $U^w : \text{IR}^3_+ \to \text{IR}$ given by

$U^w(x_t, x_{t+1}, \ell_t) = u^w(x_t, x_{t+1}) - v(\ell_t)$. His current notional commodity demand x_w^* and his notional labour supply ℓ^* are a solution of

$$\max_{x_t, l_t} u^w [x_t, (w_t \ell_t - p_t x_t)/p_{t+1}^e] - v(\ell_t) \text{ such that } w_t \ell_t - p_t x_t > 0$$

where w_t is the current nominal wage rate and p_{t+1}^e is the point forecast for the price in $t+1$.

Assumption C2

u^w and v are twice continuously differentiable. v is convex and non-decreasing for $0 < \ell < L$. u^w is strictly concave, strictly monotonically increasing with $\partial^2 u^w / \partial x_t \partial x_{t+1} > 0$. For any sequence $(x_t^n, x_{t+1}^n) \gg 0$ converging to (x_t, x_{t+1})

$$\partial u^w / \partial x_t \, (x_t^n, x_{t+1}^n) \to + \infty \qquad \text{if } x_t = 0$$
$$\partial u^w / \partial x_{t+1} \, (x_t^n, x_{t+1}^n) \to + \infty \qquad \text{if } x_{t+1} = 0$$

Let $\ell^* = a(p_t, p_{t+1}^e, w_t)$ denote the notional labour supply function. Because of the separability of workers' preferences the notional commodity demand function c^w and the notional money demand function m^w can be written as

$$x_w^* = c^w (p_t, p_{t+1}^e, W_t)$$
$$m_w^* = m^w (p_t, p_{t+1}^e, W_t)$$

where $W_t = w_t \, a (p_t, p_{t+1}^e, w_t)$. It is straightforward to demonstrate the following lemma.

Lemma 3.2

Assumption C2 implies that for all $(p_t, p_{t+1}^e, w_t) \gg 0$,

(i) $c^w (p_t, p_{t+1}^e, W_t) > 0$
$a (p_t, p_{t+1}^e, w_t) > 0$
$m^w (p_t, p_{t+1}^e, W_t) > 0$

(ii) c^w, a and m^w are differentiable functions

(iii) $\dfrac{\partial [w_t \, a \, (p_t, p_{t+1}^e, w_t)]}{\partial w_t} > 0$

$$0 \; < \; p_t \, \frac{\partial c^w}{\partial w_t} \; < \; 1$$

$$0 \; < \; \frac{\partial m^w}{\partial W_t} \; < \; 1 \, .$$

One of the important ingredients of a model where agents make intertemporal decisions is a description of how price expectations are formed (for an extensive discussion see for example Grandmont, 1977a, 1982a, 1983). The usual assumption is that agents make price forecasts on the basis of past and current prices. If such a dependence is 'too flexible' then, in general, temporary Walrasian equilibria for exchange economies may fail to exist. The usual assumption to avoid such non-existence phenomena is to impose bounds on expected prices. For the model presented here, which includes production and government activities, the restrictions on expectations can be relaxed if some additional assumptions on government activities are imposed. With these, continuity of price expectations will suffice to prove existence. This means, in particular, that price expectations may be unit elastic or even strongly inflationary. It will be assumed that price expectations of young consumers are given by continuous functions $\psi^i : \mathrm{IR}_{++} \to \mathrm{IR}_{++}$, i = w, s, which associate with each positive current price p_t a positive expected price $p_{t+1}^e, \; = \psi^i \, (p_t)$, i = w, s.

The structure of the production sector of the economy is the same as in section 3.1. Let $F : \mathrm{IR}_+ \to \mathrm{IR}_+$ denote the production function of the single profit maximizing firm. Let $h \, (w_t/p_t)$ denote notional labour demand, $F[h(w_t/p_t)]$ notional commodity supply and $\pi \, (p_t, \, w_t) = p_t \, F \, [h(w_t/p_t)] - w_t \, h \, (w_t/p_t)$ the associated profit function.

Assumption F1

$F : \mathrm{IR}_+ \to \mathrm{IR}_+$ is twice continuously differentiable, strictly monotonic and strictly concave, and

(i) $F'(0) = + \infty$ \qquad and $F'(\infty) = 0$,

(ii) $F'(\ell) \, \ell$ \quad is non-decreasing.

F1 (i) states the well-known Inada conditions, which imply that $h(w_t/p_t) > 0$ and $\Pi(p_t, w_t) > 0$ for all $(p_t, w_t) \gg 0$, and that $h(w_t/p_t) \to \infty$ as $w_t/p_t \to 0$. Assumption (ii) implies that the labour share in output does not decrease if employment increases.

The preceding description of the model generates the following aggregate excess demand functions for the commodity market and the labour market:

$$D\ (p_t, w_t, M_t, g, \tau)\ =\ \frac{M_t}{p_t} + c^w\ [p_t, \psi^w\ (p_t), w_t] +$$
$$c^s[p_t, \psi^s\ (p_t), (1 - \tau)\ \pi\ (p_t, w_t)] + g - F\ [h\ (w_t/p_t)] \quad (3.10)$$

$$Z\ (p_t, w_t) = h\ (w_t/p_t) - a\ (p_t, \psi^w\ (p_t), w_t). \qquad (3.11)$$

The two excess demand functions display some asymmetry. Since neither producers nor young workers have initial wealth, the excess demand on the labour market is independent of wealth for period t. Also, since government activity consists of commodity purchases and taxation of shareholders only, labour market excess demand is independent of government parameters as well. Both of these features are not uncommon in macroeconomic models. They facilitate the analysis substantially, but are not crucial for the results.

A temporary Walrasian equilibrium for a given triple (M_t, g, τ) is a pair $(p_t^*, w_t^*) \gg 0$ such that

$$Z\ (p_t^*, w_t^*) = 0$$

$$D\ (p_t^*, w_t^*, M_t, g, \tau) = 0 \qquad\qquad\qquad (3.12)$$

Some remarks are in order concerning the existence of such an equilibrium. It is clear that government demand g cannot be arbitrarily large, since feasibility requires that $g < F(\bar{L})$, which is the maximal producible output of the economy. On the other hand, since price expectations are not necessarily bounded, a positive tax rate has to be used as a wedge between real income and real demand by young consumers in order to clear the commodity market. Theorem 3.1 summarizes these arguments and establishes the existence of a temporary Walrasian equilibrium.

Theorem 3.1

If the assumptions C1, C2 and F1 hold, then there exists a positive constant $K > 0$ such that there exists a temporary Walrasian equilibrium $(p_t^*, w_t^*) \gg 0$ for every (M_t, g, τ) with $M_t > 0$ and $g < \tau K$.

As is to be expected from standard equilibrium theory, much stronger assumptions are required to establish uniqueness of a temporary Walrasian equilibrium. Although uniqueness is not an essential feature for the subsequent discussion of temporary equilibria with quantity rationing, it facilitates the analysis considerably and it provides a convenient geometric representation. For situations with multiple equilibria, no essential difficulties arise. However, the analysis would be much more complex. This applies in particular to the dynamic properties of non-stationary equilibria with quantity rationing.

In order to motivate the set of additional sufficient assumptions for uniqueness used in theorem 3.2 below, a brief discussion of the problem may be helpful. It is straightforward to show using the assumptions C1, C2 and F1 that for every positive current price p_t there exists a unique wage rate $w_t > 0$ which clears the labour market alone. Hence, there exists a well-defined function $\mu : \mathrm{IR}_{++} \to \mathrm{IR}_{++}$ such that $w_t = \mu(p_t)$ and

$$h\left[\mu(p_t)/p_t\right] = a\left[p_t,\, \psi^w(p_t),\, \mu(p_t)\right] \text{ for all } p_t > 0.$$

Moreover, there exist $0 < \underline{a} < \bar{a}$ which are lower and upper bounds for the real wage, i.e. $\underline{a} \leqslant \mu(p_t)/p_t \leqslant \bar{a}$.

Suppressing the time index for the remaining discussion, define

$$\alpha = \tilde{\mu}(p) = \mu(p)/p$$
$$\theta^i(p) = \psi^i(p)/p \qquad i = w, s.$$

Then the excess demand on the commodity market under labour market clearing can be written as

$$\tilde{D}(p) = \frac{M}{p} + g + c^w\left[1,\, \theta^w(p),\, \tilde{\mu}(p)\right]$$

$$+ c^s\left\{1,\, \theta^s(p),\, (1-\tau)\,\pi\left[1,\, \tilde{\mu}(p)\right]\right\} - F\left[h\left(\tilde{\mu}(p)\right)\right].$$

Taking the derivative with respect to p yields

$$\tilde{D}'(p) = -\frac{M}{p^2} + \frac{d\theta^w}{dp}\frac{\partial c^w}{\partial \theta^w} + \frac{d\theta^s}{dp}\frac{\partial c^s}{\partial \theta^s}$$

$$+ \tilde{\mu}'\left\{ \frac{\partial c^w}{\partial \alpha} - \frac{\partial c^s}{\partial \pi}(1-\tau)\,h\,[\tilde{\mu}(p)] \right.$$

$$\left. - \tilde{\mu}(p)\,h'\,[\tilde{\mu}(p)] \right\}$$

C1, C2 and F1 imply that the expression in braces is positive. Moreover, from labour market clearing $h(\alpha) - a(1, \theta^w, \alpha) = 0$ one has

$$\tilde{\mu}'(p) = \frac{(\partial a/\partial \theta^w)\,(d\theta^w/dp)}{h'(\alpha) - \partial a/\partial \alpha}.$$

Therefore, for example, if price expectations are unit elastic, i.e. if $d\theta^i/dp = 0$ for i = w,s, then the temporary Walrasian equilibrium is unique, since then $\tilde{D}' < 0$. In this case the cross price effects of consumers play no role. However, if consumer preferences exhibit a strong substitution effect, i.e. a non-positively sloped offer curve between current and future consumption, then the assumption on price expectations can be weakened. This simply expresses the fact that the right interplay of intertemporal preferences and price expectations is responsible for a downward-sloping excess demand function $\tilde{D}(p)$. The following assumptions represent only one possibility for obtaining uniqueness.

Assumption C3

$$-\frac{[\partial^2 u^i/\partial(x_{t+1})^2]x_{t+1}}{\partial u^i/\partial x_{t+1}} \leq 1 \quad \text{and} \quad \frac{\partial^2 u^i}{\partial x_t\,\partial x_{t+1}} = 0 \quad i = w,s.$$

Assumption C4

For i = w,s the expectation functions are continuously differentiable such that for all $p_t > 0$

$$\frac{d\psi^i}{dp_t}\frac{p_t}{\psi^i(p_t)} \leq 1 \qquad i = w,s$$

C4 bounds the price expectations to be at most unit elastic. The first expression in C3 is the relative risk aversion of the worker with respect to future consumption. If it is less than unity, then labour supply is a decreasing function of the future price. In addition cross price effects of current consumption are positive. Together these properties imply the following uniqueness result.

Theorem 3.2

If the assumptions C1–C4 and F1 hold, then there exists at most one temporary Walrasian equilibrium for every (M_t, g, τ).

A graphical illustration of the existence problem may be obtained by analysing the labour market and the commodity market clearing situations separately. The analysis above used the fact that, for every positive price p_t, there exists a unique labour market clearing wage $w_t = \mu\,(p_t)$. Similarly, one can show that, for every $p_t > 0$, there exists a unique wage rate $w_t = \eta\,(p_t)$ which yields a zero of the commodity excess demand function (3.10). Again the associated real wage has an upper bound $\bar{\beta} \geq \eta\,(p)/p$. Under the assumptions of theorem 3.2, η is a convex function whereas μ is concave. In figure 3.4 the graphs of the two functions μ and η have been drawn with their respective upper and lower bounds $\bar{\beta}$ and $\underline{\alpha}$. $(p_t^*,\, w_t^*)$ is the unique temporary Walrasian equilibrium. On the sides of μ and η marked plus and minus there is positive or negative excess demand respectively. It follows that $\bar{\beta} < \bar{\alpha}$ occurs for g sufficiently large. Then no equilibrium exists.

Finally, at the temporary Walrasian equilibrium $(p_t^*,\, w_t^*)$ it follows from (3.10), (3.11) and from the budget constraints of the consumer that the change in the stock of money held by consumers is equal to the budget deficit, i.e.

$$M_{t+1} - M_t = (1 - \tau)\,\Pi^* + w_t^*\ell^* - p_t^*\,(x_s^* + x_w^*) + p_t^*(x_s^* + x_w^*)$$
$$+ p_t^*[g - F\,(\ell^*)]$$
$$= p_t^*g - \tau\Pi^*.$$

In general, the deficit will be different from zero. Thus arbitrary choices of government policy variables will not guarantee a balanced budget, and therefore this will imply a non-stationary process if more than one period is analysed. The money adjustment process will be analysed in chapter 5.

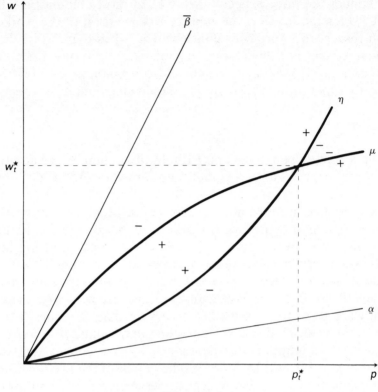

Figure 3.4

Typology of Equilibria with Quantity Rationing

For the simple macroeconomic model under consideration here, equilibria with quantity rationing at non-Walrasian prices take on the three distinct forms already characterized in section 3.1. Since the number of agents active on each side of the two markets for goods and labour services is small, the one-sidedness condition implies a very simple structure making the specification of a particular mechanism in most cases unnecessary. Moreover, since the mechanism has to be deterministic on the labour market, it will be assumed that rationing on the goods market is deterministic as well. Hence, the resulting Drèze allocations will be of the following three basic types. It is assumed of course that there is no rationing on the demand for money. Given temporary non-Walrasian prices, there are four possible combinations of rationing:

1 binding supply constraints on the labour and on the commodity market;
2 binding demand constraints on both markets;
3 binding demand constraints on the commodity market and binding supply constraints on the labour market;
4 binding demand constraints on the labour market and binding supply constraints on the commodity market.

Case (4) involves the single firm alone and it is a boundary case since profit maximization under two constraints simultaneously always makes one constraint redundant. Case (4) will appear as a non-trivial situation if the firm can hold inventories. This will make the firm's decision problem a non-trivial intertemporal one, a case which will be discussed in parts of chapter 4.

If government demand rationing is excluded, then case (3) involves consumer rationing only with the producer realizing his notional supply and demand. This case is called classical unemployment. Case (2) implies unfulfilled commodity demand and unfulfilled labour demand. This is taken as a situation of demand pressure on prices which has been termed a repressed inflation equilibrium. Finally, case (1) shows unfulfilled supplies on both markets with unemployment in the labour market due to insufficient demand in the commodity market. This situation is called Keynesian unemployment. Cases (1)–(3) involve consumer rationing in one form or another.

Keynesian Unemployment

In chapter 2 the analysis of equilibria at non-Walrasian prices was carried out taking all markets simultaneously into consideration, without paying special attention as to which side of which market had a binding constraint. In the macroeconomic context here, it is useful to analyse the three possible cases one after the other and to combine them into the full interdependent model afterwards. More specifically, for each price–wage situation, the possibilities for the existence of each of the three cases will be investigated by parametrizing the situation by alternative choices of the associated rationing constraints. For the remainder of this section the time subscript on all variables will be dropped.

Starting with the case of Keynesian unemployment, suppose that the worker consumer is facing a binding constraint z on the labour market, i.e. $0 \leqslant z < a\,[p, \psi^w\,(p), w] = \ell^*$. Then, his Drèze demand for commodities, which is equal to the Benassy effective demand for the commodity, is defined by the solution $(\tilde{x}, \tilde{\ell})$ of the problem

$$\max_{(x,\ell)} u^w\,[x, (w\ell - px)/\psi^w\,(p)] - v(\ell)$$

such that $w\ell - px \geqslant 0$ and $\ell \leqslant z$.

Because of C2, $\tilde{\ell} = z$ and $\tilde{x}$ can be written as

$$\tilde{x} = c^w\,[p, \psi^w\,(p), wz] = c_u^w\,(p, w, z), \tag{3.13}$$

which is the effective demand function for alternative rationing levels z on the labour market. For $z \geqslant \ell^*$ it follows that $c_u^w\,(p, w, z) = c^w\,[p, \psi^w\,(p), wa\,[p, \psi^w\,(p), w]]$. C2 implies that $c_u^w\,(p, w, 0) = 0$, that c_u^w is differentiable and that

$$0 < p\,\frac{\partial c_u^w}{\partial z} < w \quad \text{for} \quad z < a\,[p, \psi^w\,(p)\,w]. \tag{3.14}$$

This property states that the marginal propensity to consume out of labour income is less than unity. Define the aggregate effective commodity demand function C_u of the consumption sector as

$$C_u\,(p, w, M, \tau, z) \;=\; c_u^w\,(p, w, z) \;+\; \frac{M}{p}$$

$$+\, c^s\,\{p, \psi^s\,(p), (1 - \tau)\,[p\,F\,(z) - wz]\}. \tag{3.15}$$

It is straightforward to show that

$$0 < \frac{\partial C_u}{\partial z} < F'\,(z) \quad \text{if} \quad z < \ell^*, F'\,(z) > \frac{w}{p} \tag{3.16}$$

i.e. the aggregate marginal propensity to consume is less than the marginal product of labour calculated at the rationing level $z < \ell^*$ if the marginal product is greater than the real wage.

The effective commodity demand function of consumers C_u is the appropriate analogue of the consumption function used in the standard Keynesian model. Apart from the fact that prices and wages appear as arguments, several essential differences compared with the consumption function used in section 3.1 should be noted. First, because of the overlapping generations structure of consumers, aggregate consumption is additively separable between consumption out of accumulated real wealth and consumption out of income generated in the current period. Since young consumers possess no initial wealth, only the real balances of old consumers matter for all wealth effects. This implies in particular that, without government transfers and bequests, the quantity of money held at the end of the current period has no demand impact in the current period. Second, given the preferences of the worker, it is in general impossible to write his effective consumption demand as a function of labour income. This can only be done in the special case of separable preferences between leisure and consumption, as is assumed here. Finally, (3.15) makes apparent that the income distribution, which varies with the level of employment, and the form of the tax scheme are determining factors for the form of the aggregate consumption function. Hence, in general it is impossible to write aggregate effective consumption demand as a function of aggregate income.

Consider the supply rationed producer with a binding quantity constraint $0 \leq x < F[h(w/p)]$. Profit maximization given x implies the effective labour demand function $z = F^{-1}(x)$. Since x is binding, $F^{-1}(x) < h(w/p)$, so that $F'[F^{-1}(x)] > w/p$ for all $0 \leq x < F[h(w/p)]$. Hence, for each supply rationing situation of the producer, his effective labour demand implies a marginal product greater than the real wage.

It is now straightforward to define an equilibrium of Keynesian unemployment using the new concept of the aggregate effective demand.

Definition 3.2

For a given list (M_t, g, τ), a triple (p, w, L) of prices, wages and employment is a Keynesian unemployment equilibrium denoted K if

$$C_u(p, w, M, \tau, L) = F(L) - g$$
$$L < h(w/p) \text{ and } L < a[p, \psi^w(p), w]. \tag{3.17}$$

Figure 3.5 gives a characterization of (3.17) where $z^* = h(w/p)$ is the notional labour demand.

Lemma 3.3

If the assumptions C1, C2 and F1 hold, then any Keynesian equilibrium is unique if $(M, g) \neq 0$.

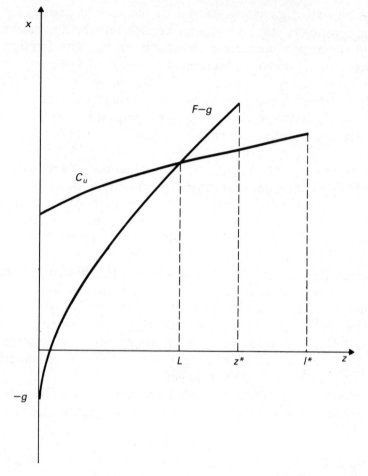

Figure 3.5

The uniqueness follows directly from (3.16) and from the fact that $C_u (p, w, M, \tau, 0) = M/p$.

Repressed Inflation

Consider a demand rationing situation on the commodity market. Since the four private agents and the government are active on the demand side of the commodity market, a rationing scheme has to distribute the available supply among the five agents. It is clear that different schemes will yield different equilibria for the same list (p, w, M_i, g, τ) and that multiplicity of equilibria may arise for a particular rationing scheme. Before dealing with these issues, the behaviour of young agents under demand rationing will be described.

Let $0 \leqslant x_w < x_w^*$ denote the level of commodity rationing for a young worker which he takes as given (i.e. non-manipulable). The optimal decision consists of the solution $(\tilde{x}, \tilde{\ell})$ of the problem

$$\max_{(x,\ell)} u^w[x, (w\ell - px)/\psi^w(p)] - v(\ell)$$

such that $w\ell - px \geqslant 0$ and $x \leqslant x_w$.

Assumption C2 implies that $\tilde{x} = x_w$ and that $\tilde{\ell}$ is a continuously differentiable function $\tilde{\ell} = a_x(p,w,x_w)$. a_x describes effective labour supply under demand rationing of the worker, i.e. the spillover effect from the commodity market to the labour market. It follows from C2 that $a_x(p,w,0) > 0$ and $\partial a_x/\partial x_w > 0$ for all $(p,w) \geqslant 0$ and $0 \leqslant x_w < x_w^*$.

Rationing of the shareholder at a level x_s will imply that he will purchase exactly this amount at the given net profit π, increasing savings for more consumption in the second period of his life. For the producer labour demand rationing at a level $0 \leqslant z < h[w(p)]$ means that he will employ the level z and supply $F(z)$.

The rationing mechanism on the commodity market serves the government and old consumers first. Any positive amount $\tilde{X}$ left is divided between the young worker and shareholder. Therefore the demand constraints x_w and x_s can be written as $x_w = \varphi(\tilde{X})$, $x_s = \tilde{X} - \varphi(\tilde{X})$ where $\varphi: \mathbb{R}_+ \to \mathbb{R}_+$ with $\varphi(\tilde{X}) \leqslant \tilde{X}$. Given (p,w) and (M,g,τ) a repressed inflation equilibrium for the rationing scheme φ is characterized by a pair $(x_w, L) \geqslant 0$ of consumption and labour by the worker such that

(i) $F(L) - g - M/p - x_w \leqslant c^s \{p, \psi^s(p), (1 - \tau)[pF(L) - wL]\}$

(ii) $L = a_x(p,w,x_w) < h(w/p)$

(iii) $x_w < c^w[p,\psi^w(p),w]$ (3.18)

(iv) $[F(L) - g - M/p] x_w \geqslant 0$

(v) $x_w = \varphi[\max\{0, F(L) - g - M/p\}]$.

The conditions (i)–(iii) characterize feasibility and demand rationing, whose set of solutions (if non-empty) will be a continuum in general. This clearly indicates the need for some specification which is given by (iv) and (v). Condition (iv) stipulates that young consumers are rationed to zero as long as the government and old consumers have not been satisfied.

The technique developed for the Keynesian case which described a relationship between aggregate private consumption and labour will prove useful here as well. To reduce the amount of notation, (p,w) will be suppressed as arguments for all functions for the remainder of this section. Let $X \geq 0$ denote any possible supply to private consumers after government demand has been satisfied. Then, given the rationing mechanism φ, effective labour supply can be written as a function of aggregate private consumption given by

$$A_x(X) = \min\{a_x[\varphi(\max\{0, X - M/p\})], \ell^*\}.$$

This allows us to rewrite definition (3.18) of a repressed inflation equilibrium in terms of aggregates. A pair $(L,X) \geq 0$ of employment and private consumption is an equilibrium of repressed inflation if

(i) $\max \{0,F(L) - g\} = X < x_w^* + x_s^* + M/p$

(ii) $L = A_x(X) < h(w/p).$ \hfill (3.19)

The definition does not specify how rationing will be divided between the government and the old consumers. However, the rationing mechanism φ stipulates that this will occur when young consumers are rationed at a zero level. Choosing φ appropriately, one obtains a similar uniqueness result here as for the Keynesian situation.

Lemma 3.4

If the assumptions C1, C2 and F1 hold, then there exists a rationing scheme φ such that for any $(p,w) \gg 0$ there exists at most one inflationary equilibrium.

It is clear that the properties of the production function and of consumer preferences play an important role in determining the particular rationing scheme φ which guarantees uniqueness. In general, however, there are many such schemes. With some additional assumptions on preferences (homotheticity and separability, for example), the uniform proportional mechanism may be among the admissible ones.

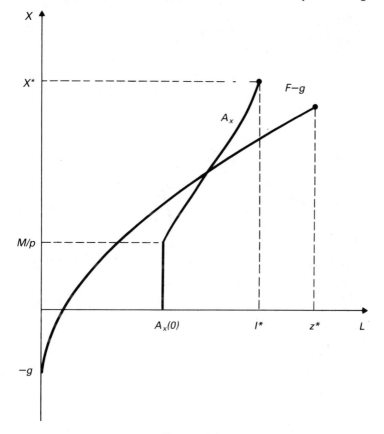

Figure 3.6

A consequence of the uniqueness result is that the function $F[A_x(X)] - g - X$ has at most one zero. Combined with the fact that $A_x(0) > 0$, this implies that $F'A'_x - 1 < 0$ at any inflationary state with $X > 0$. Figure 3.6 provides a geometric characterisation of a repressed inflation equilibrium. The graphs of the two functions $F - g$ and A_x are represented in the same coordinate space as in figure 3.5 with X on the vertical axis and L on the horizontal axis. $X^* = M/p + x^*_w + x^*_s$ is the unconstrained private consumption demand.

Classical Unemployment

The third possible case leaves the producer unrationed whilst imposing demand constraints on consumers and unemployment for the worker. Using the concepts of the two preceding cases,

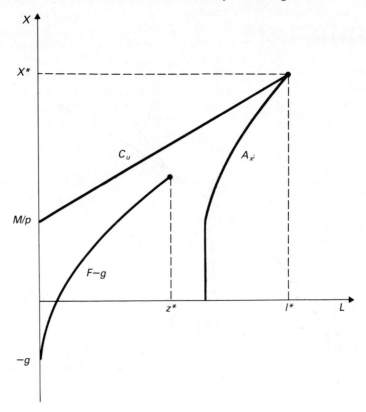

Figure 3.7

classical unemployment states are defined in a straightforward way.

Definition 3.3

Given (M,g,τ) and $(p,w) \geqslant 0$, a pair (L,X) is a classical unemployment situation if

(i) $h(w/p) = L < A_x(p,w,M,\tau,X)$

(3.20)

(ii) $F[h(w/p)] - g = X < C_u(p,w,M,\tau,L)$.

On both markets the spillovers due to the rationing are larger than the realization, leaving unsatisfied supplies and demands respectively. Figure 3.7 provides a geometric characterization which combines the features of the two preceding diagrams.

3.3 Comparative Statics

Combining the elements of the model described for the three distinct possible cases one obtains a uniform description of the type of equilibrium and its associated activity levels (L,X) for each given pair of prices and wages (p,w), total wealth of old consumers M and policy variables (g,τ). The assumptions made so far guarantee that there exists a unique allocation for each $(p,w) \gg 0$ (for a proof see Böhm, 1978). Hence, there exists a continuous function $L = \mathscr{L}(p,w,M,g,\tau)$ which yields the employment level L for each acceptable quintuple (p,w,M,g,τ). As a consequence the uniqueness determines a partition of the price-wage space into the three different regions of Keynesian unemployment K, classical unemployment C and repressed inflation I. Therefore, $\mathscr{L}$ allows all non-Walrasian allocations to be characterized for a given history of the economy specified by the wealth of old consumers and for current government control variables g and τ. A schematic representation of the partition of (p,w)-space is given in figure 3.8. Its precise characteristics depend of course on more specific properties of the underlying microeconomic data of the economy, which can be derived from the assumptions. Figure 3.8 also contains three different level sets of the function $\mathscr{L}$, i.e. the so-called isoemployment curves. These are closed curves centred around the Walrasian price–wage pair (p^*, w^*) with the maximal employment level at (p^*, w^*).

Comparing figure 3.2 with figure 3.8, the main qualitative difference is that the boundary between the regions K and I is no longer a vertical line. This feature stems exclusively from the fact that notional labour supply is not exogenous. Along $I \cap K$ consumers are not rationed. Therefore, the slope of this boundary depends on preferences of workers as well as on the technology. In general, there is no reason why this boundary should be downward sloping. For example, in the model by Malinvaud (1977) the boundary is positively sloped near the Walrasian equilibrium and negatively sloped for larger values of the commodity price.

Another difference between figure 3.2 and figure 3.8 is the shape of the isoemployment curves in the Keynesian region and in the region of repressed inflation. This reflects the different partial derivatives of the function $\mathscr{L}$ with respect to p and w.

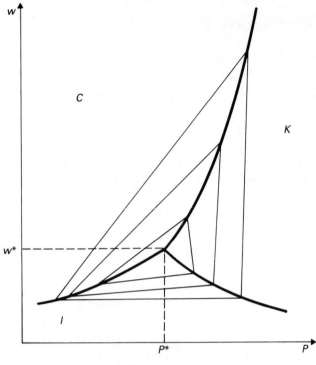

Figure 3.8

Clearly, if labour supply is exogenous, employment is maximal in the region of repressed inflation as in the IS–LM model of section 3.1. The same would be true in the prototype model, if consumer-workers supplied a fixed amount of labour. With regard to the slope of the isoemployment lines under Keynesian unemployment, the IS–LM model has no wage effect on aggregate demand. Therefore these lines must be vertical. However, in the prototype model changes in the wage rate have opposite effects on income for workers and shareholders. Therefore the effect on aggregate consumption due to a wage change depends on the difference in the marginal propensities to consume of the two young consumers.

The comparison of the allocation function $\mathscr{L}$ for the two models indicates a striking equivalence, in spite of the fact that the IS–LM model possesses a richer asset structure. It will be argued at the end of this chapter that this is always true, as long as asset markets are always in equilibrium. This makes the 'real' part of any standard Keynesian model a particular special case of some variant of the prototype model. The same holds true for the models presented by Barro and Grossman (1976), Benassy (1977a) and Malinvaud (1977). The model due to Malinvaud is the closest to the prototype model, since it also treats the case of a profits tax and an intertemporal consumer, whose behaviour could be made consistent with an overlapping generations model. Benassy deals with a completely private model without government activity. The model by Barro and Grossman assumes constant government real demand as do the model due to Malinvaud and the prototype model but introduces lump sum taxes. The differences of these models in their specification of consumer preferences are the only relevant source for minor qualitative changes in comparison with the prototype model. All of them, however, derive the same qualitative properties of a short-run allocation function $\mathcal{L}$.

Rigid Wages and Flexible Prices

Suppose that commodity prices are sufficiently flexible to clear the commodity market, i.e. at a given wage rate prices are such that there is no rationing on the commodity market. Because of the one-sidedness assumption, this leaves two possibilities of rationing on the labour market, i.e. unemployment or demand rationing of the producer. The unemployment states imply that the producer is not rationed, so that the commodity price is always such that the marginal product of labour equals the real wage. Any state (p,w) with this property belongs to $C \cap K$ or $C \cap I$, i.e. to the boundaries between the classical and the Keynesian or the classical and the inflationary regions. States belonging to $C \cap I$, however, imply demand rationing on the commodity market, contradicting the assumption of no rationing on that market. The boundary $C \cap K$ corresponds to situations where the nominal wage rate is larger than the Walrasian wage rate w^*. Hence, price flexibility cannot restore full employment, which is prevented by the downward rigidity of the nominal wage. Since there is unemployment, any conventional wage adjustment process would demand a wage decrease. Hence, one observes the typical situation originally discussed and analysed by Keynes, where a high and rigid nominal wage rate is the major cause for unemployment.

The remaining case is demand rationing on the labour market

which implies states of no consumer rationing. These are the states on the boundary between Keynesian unemployment and repressed inflation, i.e. $(p,w) \in K \cap I$. There, the marginal product of labour is larger than the real wage with demand pressure on the labour market. Hence, downward rigidity of wages alone will not allow these states to persist, implying a tendency for nominal wages to rise. Therefore any conventional wage adjustment mechanism will eventually eliminate these states, leaving unemployment states as the only ones to remain under downward wage rigidity.

The complete description of the model reveals some additional insights into the effectiveness of wage and price policies which is usually not apparent in macroeconomic models describing unemployment situations. The general conclusion that lower wages imply higher levels of employment is not universally true in all unemployment states if there is some price rigidity as well. Whereas employment can be improved in all classical states by lowering the wage rate and/or increasing prices, employment increases in Keynesian states may require the opposite changes in prices and wages. Figure 3.8 reveals the essential features. Since there exists excess supply on the commodity market lower prices will improve employment in general. However, wage increases may be required to increase employment if, geometrically speaking, the isoemployment curves in the Keynesian region are upward sloping. The source of this property is a positive marginal propensity to consume out of wages of workers which dominates the marginal propensity to consume out of income of the shareholder, thus implying a positive change on aggregate effective demand. This possibility is revealed by most economists using the deterministic framework (see for example Malinvaud, 1977). Its appearance is in no way related to degenerate cases only.

Government Policies

Short-run effects of government policy changes can be described using the same comparative statics methods as above by analysing the properties of the function $\mathscr{L}$. Since the model does not contain a bond market a monetary policy would be equivalent to direct monetary transfer payments, i.e. free gifts to consumers. Although such transfers could easily be included in the model here, its treatment would not reveal the essential features of a monetary policy as conceptualized in traditional Keynesian theory. Moreover, the overlapping generations structure implies that total wealth in each period is the result of savings behaviour of young consumers in the preceding period. These arguments imply that for the present model changes of government demand g and of the tax rate τ constitute the only government policy variables, leaving monetary policy issues to a later chapter where a bond market has been added to the model.

The comparative static effects of an increase in government purchases at given (p,w) are obtained directly from the definitions (3.17), (3.19) and (3.20). Let $y = F(L)$ denote total output. Then the employment and output multipliers for the regimes C, K and I are given by

$$\left.\frac{dL}{dg}\right|_C = \left.\frac{dy}{dg}\right|_C = 0$$

$$\left.\frac{dL}{dg}\right|_K = \frac{1}{F' - \partial C_u/\partial L} ;$$

$$\left.\frac{dy}{dg}\right|_K = \frac{F'}{F' - \partial C_u/\partial L} > 1 \tag{3.21}$$

$$\left.\frac{dL}{dg}\right|_I = \frac{-\partial A_x/\partial X}{1 - F' \cdot (\partial A_x/\partial X)} \leqslant 0 ;$$

$$\left.\frac{dy}{dg}\right|_I = \frac{-F' \cdot (\partial A_x/\partial X)}{1 - F' \cdot (\partial A_x/\partial X)} \leqslant 0 .$$

The tax multipliers have the opposite signs. Clearly, increased government demand has no employment and no output effect under classical unemployment, implying more severe demand rationing for consumers. The presence of demand rationing on the commodity market in inflationary states yields the negative multipliers and therefore also increased demand rationing. The multipliers are zero whenever young consumers are rationed to zero already. Finally, the Keynesian multipliers are of the expected sign and the output multiplier is greater than unity, confirming the traditional intuition that each additional unit spent by the government creates a positive multiple in total income, due to a positive marginal propensity to consume which is less than unity.

The effects on the government deficit and thus on the change $M_{t+1} - M_t$ of the money stock under Keynesian unemployment can be deduced directly. Let

$$\Delta = \tau[pF(L) - wL] - pg \tag{3.22}$$

denote the government deficit. Then (3.22) together with (3.21) yields

$$\left.\frac{d\Delta}{dg}\right|_K = p \left[\tau \frac{F' - w/p}{F' - \partial C_u/\partial L} - 1 \right] < 0$$

$$\text{for all } 0 \leqslant \tau \leqslant 1. \tag{3.23}$$

Hence, the additional purchases always imply deficit spending for the case of a proportional profits tax even under the most severe taxation of 100 per cent. Equation (3.23) reveals that the marginal profit resulting from increased government purchases is always less than unity, in spite of the fact that the output multiplier is larger than unity. Under a general proportional income tax the deficit multiplier may be positive, zero or negative, depending on the tax rate, the marginal propensity to consume and the production function.

Apart from the effects on employment, output and the deficit, a change in government purchases implies a displacement of the Walrasian equilibrium (p^*, w^*) as well as of the three different regions in (p,w)-space. Consider first the dislocation of the Walrasian equilibrium. From the discussion preceding theorem 3.2 it follows that the labour market clearing locus $w = \mu(p)$ is independent of any government parameters. Hence, any Walrasian equilibrium has to lie on μ. Moreover, employment decreases or increases along μ as the real wage $\mu(p)/p$ increases or decreases, i.e. the full employment trade-off is determined by the convexity or concavity of μ. Assumptions C1–C4 and F1 imply that μ is concave, and strictly concave if price expectations are strictly less than unit elastic.

Consider the notional excess demand on the commodity

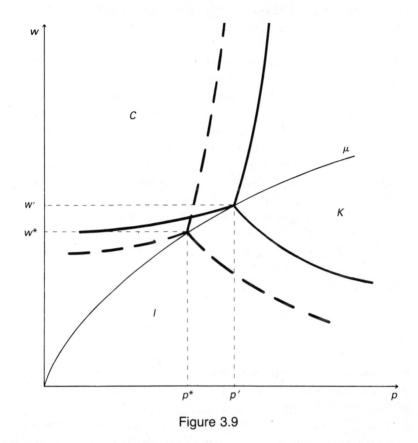

Figure 3.9

market $D(p,w,g)$ from (3.10). $D(p^*,w^*,g) = 0$ and g' larger than g implies positive excess demand, i.e. $D(p^*,w^*,g') > 0$. Therefore, $g' > g$ implies that the new Walrasian equilibrium must have higher prices $p' > p^*$ and higher wages $w' > w^*$. If price expectations of workers are unit elastic, then labour supply is a function of the real wage alone and the labour market clearing real wage is a given constant. Hence, all full-employment levels are the same. However, if price expectations are less than unit elastic, then μ is strictly concave and $g' > g$ implies $w^*/p^* > w'/p'$. Hence, the temporary Walrasian equilibrium with the larger government demand must have a higher level of full employment.

A geometric characterization of the effect of increasing government purchases from g to g' is given in figure 3.9. The diagram shows that the region of repressed inflation is enlarged, including states which were previously classical and Keynesian. Thus increasing government purchases increases the potential for demand rationing on the commodity market. All classical states at the outset will be either classical or inflationary afterwards. Conversely, some Keynesian states will change to classical and some to inflationary states, among them the original Walrasian equilibrium (p^*, w^*).

For a complete understanding of the effectiveness of fiscal policies, the short-run effects discussed so far have to be supplemented by the effects on the amount of money held by consumers. As was indicated, the government budget constraint implies such effects and it would be wrong to ignore them – a tradition, however, that was maintained by macroeconomists for a long time. Blinder and Solow (1973, 1974) and Tobin and Buiter (1976) present the necessary modifications within the standard IS–LM model. For the prototype model here, this will be carried out in detail in chapter 5.

3.4 Concluding Remarks

The goal of this chapter was threefold. The lessons from Walrasian and non-Walrasian theory have demonstrated that it should be possible to design a consistent microeconomic general equilibrium model with a macroeconomic flavour. The overlapping generations structure is a natural choice in order to model dynamic phenomena and intertemporal utility maximizing choices of individual agents. It was shown that the notion of an equilibrium with quantity rationing provides a description of states with involuntary unemployment, and that the traditional Keynesian short-run model is structurally equivalent to the prototype model. It is clear that many important features, which have been treated already in the literature of the theory of non-Walrasian allocations, are missing. Many of them are discussed in chapter 2. The strictly deterministic and non-strategic structure has to be extended. But is seems that a model like the one presented here will always serve as a point of reference.

One advantage of starting with a consistent microeconomic model is that it supplies unambiguous restrictions for aggregate effective demand and supply functions. These should be taken into account in the formulation of aggregate functions. Here it became clear that the standard Keynesian model lacked some microeconomic consistency.

Most importantly, however, the structural equivalence of the real parts of the prototype model and of the Keynesian model show that the richer asset market structure in the latter has no decisive influence on the real part of the economy. In other words, the assumption of market clearing on all asset markets in such models induces the same allocative features as a model with money alone. Bonds and other financial assets therefore play an important role in the portfolio decisions of private agents and the financing possibilities of the government. However, their influence on real phenomena is 'washed out' through the equilibrium conditions on all asset markets. Hence, the 'real' part of the prototype model contains and displays all relevant features of a more extended model. Clearly, this should not be taken to imply that asset markets do not matter for the type of disequilibrium allocations. In particular, comparative static as well as dynamic effects of government policy depend crucially on asset market possibilities. Further research with more extended models has to show how far this separation of real and financial phenomena can be maintained.

4

Beyond the Prototype: Extensions and Generalizations

Section 3.2 presented a prototype model which provides the methodological basis and a general structure for a consistent macroeconomic analysis under non-market clearing conditions. The model allowed a comprehensive view of the two distinct situations of classical and of Keynesian unemployment. Certainly, many important macroeconomic problems cannot be treated using the simple prototype model, since they require substantial extensions. However, some of these are straightforward in the sense that, for their introduction into the model, existing elements of partial equilibrium theories can be added without any major difficulty. The research of the past decade provides some of these extensions. Before describing a few of them in detail, it may be of some interest to list the most obvious and direct ones. This, in effect, amounts to a description of a possible research programme.

One of the most important extensions is clearly the incorporation of capital investment and/or inventory holding. Traditional investment and production theory serves as a starting point to discuss and describe the role of expectations in determining the level of employment. The inventory case will be treated below. Enlarging the spectrum of financial assets to government bonds as well as to credit would make the model amenable to the treatment of many of the controversial issues in macroeconomics over the effectiveness or neutrality of alternative economic policies: (a) the influence of government debt on unemployment; (b) the question of debt versus money as a means to finance government expenditures; (c) the effectiveness of alternative tax schemes. It seems straightforward to include exogenous uncertainty in the model, thus providing a framework for a discussion of rational expectations equilibria under non-market clearing conditions.

Last but not least, the explicit modelling of consumer preferences allows a welfare analysis of different government policies. In particular an analysis of steady states yields a description of intergenerational trade-offs and other problems like the cost or gains from inflation.

4.1 Inventories

The macroeconomic model described in chapter 3 contains an essential asymmetry between households and the single firm. While the former are confronted with an intertemporal decision problem, the firm maximizes short-run profits using an instantaneous production function. Such a simple structure makes all intertemporal considerations of the firm superfluous. In particular, expectations concerning future prices and wages as well as future rationing on the labour and on the goods market play no role. To exclude the role of firm's expectations on current decisions from a general macroeconomic model not only is in violation of observed empirical fact, but also excludes one of the fundamental factors determining employment, an issue stressed so convincingly by Keynes.

The atemporal structure of the producer's decision problem entails a second essential restriction. Since neither storage nor investment are possible, the lack of intertemporal substitution in production reduces all short-run substitution effects across markets to the monotone relationship between input and output. This excludes a wide range of spillover effects, from the labour market to the goods market and vice versa, that are linked to buffer stocks, involuntary inventories, excess capacity and labour hoarding. Thus, some of the critique regarding the inability of the previous standard model with quantity rationing to deal with these issues at the same time points to the necessity of an appropriate extension of the model.

Two contributions (Böhm, 1980; Muellbauer and Portes, 1978) introduced inventories into the model above, implying a general structure for a discussion of the problems raised before. This richer model provides valuable insights into the nature of quantity signals and their associated spillover effects. Apart from the symmetric treatment of the behaviour of consumers and producers, the model yields a complete and non-degenerate description of the four possible disequilibrium states for the two markets. As a result, a clear distinction between states with demand rationing and those with supply rationing for the firm is obtained which gives rise to different policy effects. In spite of its additional complexity, which in some respects may be even greater than the standard IS–LM framework, the model retains a simple manageable structure as a macromodel.

The technological process of holding inventories from one period to the next is just a description of how the same physical commodity in one period can be made available in a succeeding one through production possibilities. Hence, any technology which involves a commodity at different dates describes the possibility of inventory holding. In a model with discrete time as used here, the amount of an unsold stock of commodities, i.e. the inventory held, is equal to the input into the process of inventory holding. The total stock available at the next period then depends on the technology and on other inputs. Leaving aside problems of production processes which take more than one period (creating intermediate products within the firm), it will be assumed that the technology of the firm does not allow instantaneous production in the same period. Formally, its inclusion in the model would not cause any difficulties, but the qualitative properties of demand and supply decisions would always be a mixture of intertemporal and intratemporal substitution in production. Restricting the technology, however, to intertemporal production only has the advantage of bringing out the consequences of inventory holding more clearly. Therefore, the technology of the firm will be described by a production function $F : \mathbb{R}_+^2 \rightarrow \mathbb{R}_+$ which associates with every pair (z,i) of labour input $z \geq 0$ and inventory (commodity) input $i \geq 0$ a total stock of commodities $\omega = F(z,i)$ available at the beginning of the succeeding period. It is immediate that a production plan with zero labour input $(0,i)$ would be called a pure storage activity, and, in general, one may have $F(0,i) \gtreqless i$ depending on whether the function F describes natural growth or decay. In special cases F may be additively separable implying that storage and new production are two independent activities. As will be shown below, separability implies very special spillover effects. However, for the description of the general model no such specification is needed, and it is only necessary that F is well behaved as stated in the next assumption.

Assumption F2

$F : \mathbb{R}^2_+ \to \mathbb{R}_+$ is twice continuously differentiable and strictly concave with $F(0,0) = 0$ and

(i) $\frac{\partial F}{\partial z}(z,i) = F_z(z,i) > 0$ and $\frac{\partial F}{\partial i}(z,i) = F_i(z,i) > 0$

$$\text{for all } (z,i) \geqslant 0$$

(ii) $\lim_{z \to 0} F_z(z,i) = + \infty$ for every $i \geqslant 0$

Let $\omega_0 \geqslant 0$ denote the stock of goods available to the firm at the beginning of the period, which is the result of the production decision taken in the previous period. Let $\Pi \geqslant 0$ denote profit payments to the young shareholder and $m_0 \geqslant 0$ the amount of money held by the firm at the beginning of the period. If the firm sells the amount $y \geqslant 0$ of commodities and hires the amount $z \geqslant 0$ of labour, then the firm's budget constraint becomes

$$m_0 + py = \Pi + wz + m$$

where m is the final money holding of the firm. If there is no credit and since the firm cannot sell more than it has available as stock, $m \geqslant 0$ and $\omega_0 \geqslant y$ must hold. Writing $y = \omega_0 - i$ with $i \geqslant 0$ one obtains

$$p\omega_0 + m_0 - \Pi = m + (pi + wz),$$

i.e. net wealth (total wealth minus payments to shareholders) is equal to money savings plus production cost. The equation makes apparent that the value of inventory is a part of the intertemporal production cost, but also equal to revenue forgone in the current period. Since any input decision (z,i) implies a planned output $\omega = F(z,i)$ a feasible plan of the firm in terms of planned output ω and final money holdings m has to satisfy

$$m + C(\omega,p,w) \leqslant p\omega_0 + m_0 - \Pi$$

where C is the usual cost funtion derived from F. If the firm chooses to store all its stock ω_0, then current revenue will be zero and profit payments plus wages cannot exceed initial money balances. Moreover, since the amount of commodity input cannot be larger than ω_0, the upper bound of the budget set for large output is defined by the restricted cost function with labour as the only variable input. The following lemma states the essential property of the choice set of the firm under an additional assumption which avoids bankruptcy of the firm.

Lemma 4.1

If assumption F2 is satisfied and if $(\omega_0, m_0 - \Pi) \gg 0$, then for every $(p, w) \gg 0$ the budget set

$$\{(\omega, m) \in \mathbb{R}^2_+ \,|\, \omega = F(z, i),\ 0 \leqslant i \leqslant \omega_0,\ m + pi + wz \leqslant p\omega_0 + m_0 - \Pi\}$$

is non-empty and strictly convex at all $(\omega, m) \gg 0$.

Figure 4.1 provides a geometric characterization. At the point $\tilde{\omega}$, the input restriction $i \leqslant \omega_0$ becomes binding, so that the frontier must coincide with the restricted cost function for $\omega > \tilde{\omega}$.

To complete the description of the behaviour of the firm the objective function has to be characterized. Once the atemporal framework of the theory of the firm is no longer valid, there exists no generally accepted objective function which describes the

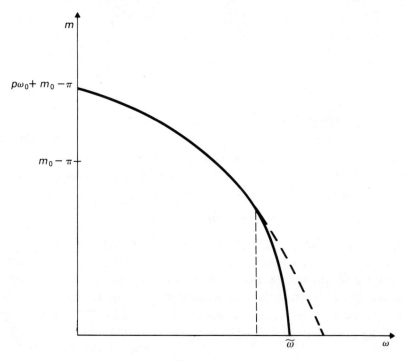

Figure 4.1

preferences of the firm. With overlapping generations of identical shareholders who own the firm essentially only during one period of their lives, it is not unreasonable to assume that the objective is independent of the preferences and situation of a particular generation. Since the payments to shareholders are made from the wealth of the firm before it decides on its new production plan, the influence of a shareholder on the behaviour of the firm in a particular period can be neglected, avoiding the difficulties of an intergenerational bargaining problem. However, since shareholder's utility depends primarily on the payments of the firm and since these have to be financed from accumulated wealth, the firm's objective function should be monotonically increasing in final money and planned output.

In order to keep the amount of uncertainty about the future for the firm at the same level as that for consumers, it will be assumed that the firm makes a point forecast on future prices and wages which depends on current prices and wages. Concerning expectations about possible rationing in the future the firm will assume that the future rationing situation will be of the same type as in the current period. The change of the expected level of rationing due to a change in current rationing can then be used as an indicator of whether the firm's expectations can be classified as optimistic or pessimistic. It is then possible to distinguish different situations and analyse how the effects of government policies depend on expectations. This will be done for the case of Keynesian unemployment at the end of this section after the general model has been presented.

Assume that the objective function of the firm is separable in output and money and consider first the situation of no rationing in the current period. Then, given price and wage expectations the objective function is assumed to be of the form $V(\omega,p,w,x,\ell) + m$ where the pair (x,ℓ) describes non-binding quantity signals for the commodity and for the labour market respectively. Since (x,ℓ) is not binding, V is constant for any small changes of the two signals and depends only on $(\omega,p,w,)$. If there is supply rationing for the firm in the current period then x is the rationing level on the commodity market. Similarly, for the case of demand rationing on the labour market, ℓ is the level of labour input at which the firm is rationed. If there is no rationing, the firm's notional commodity supply y^* and its notional labour demand z^* are obtained as a solution of

$$\max \ V(\omega,p,w,x,\ell) + m \ \text{subject to}$$
$$\omega = F(z,\omega_0 - y); \quad \omega_0 - y \geqslant 0 \tag{4.1}$$
$$m + wz \leqslant py + m_0 - \Pi.$$

Let $G(p,w,m_0,\omega_0) = y^*$ and $H(p,w,m_0,\omega_0) = z^*$ denote the respective notional supply and demand functions.

Assumption F3

V is twice continuously differentiable in $(\omega,p,w,x.\ell)$ whenever (x,ℓ) is not at the boundary of a rationing regime, strictly concave in ω and $\partial V/\partial \omega = V_\omega(\omega,p,w,x,\ell) > 0$ for all (ω,p,w,x,ℓ).

Assumptions F2 and F3 imply that G and H are in fact differentiable functions and that $y^* > 0$ and $z^* > 0$ for every $(p,w) \geqslant 0$.

Assume that the firm faces a supply constraint $x < y^* = G(p,w,m_0,\omega_0)$. In such a case the firm's inventory will be larger than its planned inventory $i^* = \omega_0 - y^*$. Moreover, the effective labour demand due to the supply rationing on the goods market will be given by a function $H_y(x,p,w,m_0,\omega_0) = \tilde{z}$ which is the solution of

$$\max \ V(\omega,p,w,x,\ell) + m \ \text{subject to}$$
$$\omega = F(z,\omega_0 - y); \quad \omega_0 - y \geqslant \omega_0 - x \tag{4.2}$$
$$m + wz \leqslant py + m_0 - \Pi.$$

It follows from F2 and F3 that H_y is a function and that the firm will sell precisely $y = x$ which induces an involuntary inventory of $\omega_0 - y \geqslant i^* = \omega_0 - y^*$. The function H_y is the complete analogue to the corresponding function of the consumer, describing the spillover from the commodity market to the labour market. However, here it is the demand spillover given a binding supply constraint. Clearly, if $x \geqslant y^*$, then

$$H_y(x,p,w,m_0,\omega_0) = H(p,w,m_0,\omega_0) = z^*.$$

In a similar fashion one obtains a description of the situation of excess labour demand. Suppose $\ell < z^* = H(p,w,m_0,\omega_0)$ is a binding constraint for the firm on the labour market. Then the effective commodity supply of the firm on the commodity market $\tilde{y}$ is given by a function

$$\tilde{y} = G_z(\ell,p,w,m_0,\omega_0)$$

which is the solution of the problem

$$\max\ V(\omega,p,w,x,\ell) + m \text{ subject to}$$
$$\omega = F(z,\omega_0 - y); \quad \omega_0 - y \geq 0; \quad z \leq \ell \qquad (4.3)$$
$$m + wz \leq py + m_0 - \Pi.$$

As before it follows from F2 and F3 that G_z is a function and that labour demand z of the firm is equal to the rationing constraint ℓ. If the rationing constraint ℓ is not binding, i.e. if $\ell > z^* = H(p,w,m_0,\omega_0)$, then effective commodity supply is equal to the notional supply.

Finally, as a fourth possible rationing situation, (x,ℓ) may be such that both constraints are binding. This occurs if

$$x < G_z(\ell,p,w,\omega_0,m_0)$$
$$\ell < H_y(x,p,w,\omega_0,m_0).$$

In this case labour demand is equal to ℓ and commodity supply is equal to x, leaving excess demand on the labour market and involuntary stocks of the commodity.

The preceding analysis indicates that, once inventories are introduced, the behaviour of the firm under alternative rationing situations can be described by the two functions G_z and H_y which describe the spillover effects from one market to the other under the two alternative rationing situations. Thus, as in the case for consumers, the two effective supply and demand functions contain all the information concerning the behaviour of the firm in a particular period. Figure 4.2 gives a geometric characterization of the two functions in the space (ℓ,x) of labour demand and sales for given prices and wages and the initial condition $(\omega_0,m_0 - \Pi)$.

It is now straightforward to define the four disequilibrium states for the model with inventories. The initial data for the given period consist of a price wage pair (p,w) and a list $(M,g,\tau,\omega_0,m_0,\Pi)$. Since the profit payments Π to shareholders are made at the beginning of the period, the shareholder's net income will be independent of the level of employment or sales. This implies no qualitative change for the two aggregate functions C_u and A_x which will be essential in what follows. Suppressing the exogenous data and (p,w) as arguments of the respective functions, let X denote total private consumption, $Y = X + g$ total sales and L employment.

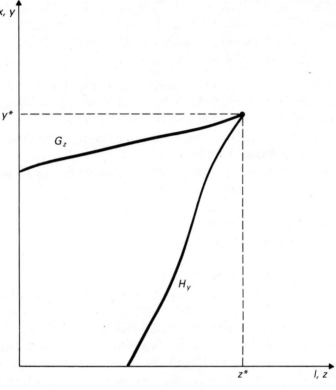

Figure 4.2

Definition 4.1

A state (L,X) is a Keynesian unemployment equilibrium K if it is a solution of

$$C_u(L) = X \qquad\qquad L < \ell^*$$
$$H_y(X + g) = L \qquad\qquad X + g < y^*.$$

Definition 4.2

A state (L, X) is a repressed inflation equilibrium I if it is a solution of

$$A_x(X) = L \qquad\qquad L < z^*$$
$$G_z(L) = X + g \qquad\qquad X < x_w^* + x_s^* + M/p.$$

Definition 4.3

A state (L, X) is a classical unemployment situation C if

$$L = H(p,w) = z^* \qquad L < A_x(X)$$
$$X + g = G(p,w) = y^* \qquad X < C_u(L).$$

Definition 4.4

A state (L, X) is an underconsumption equilibrium U if

$$L = a(p,w) = \ell^* \qquad L < H_y(X + g)$$
$$X = x_w^* + x_s^* \qquad X + g < G_z(L).$$

The state of underconsumption now replaces the boundary case $I \cap K$ of the model with instantaneous production and no inventories. It imposes a sales constraint and a labour demand constraint for the firm. Its occurrence will typically prevail for low wage rates and high prices. The essential difference of the present model compared with the simple previous one is that the firm's expectations play an important role in determining the properties of the behavioural functions G_z and H_y, their influence on the type of state which prevails at a particular price–wage pair, and the influence of government policies on employment and consumption. In order to make any comparative static analysis meaningful, it is necessary that the resulting state and allocation (L,X) is unique for the given data. Only a few additional assumptions on the micro data, in particular on firm's expectations, are required to obtain such a uniqueness result. Rather than stating these, it may be more useful to state conditions on the aggregate functions. This has the advantage of supplying a better geometric intuition of the qualitative features of the model. For the case of Keynesian unemployment, the example given below will derive the sufficient conditions from microeconomic data.

Assumption A2

Given the initial conditions $(M,g,\tau,\omega_0,m_0,\Pi)$, for every $(p,w) \gg 0$,

(i) $C_u(p,w,0) > 0 \qquad\qquad A_x(p,w,0) > 0$

(ii) $H_y(p,w,0) > 0$ $G_z(p,w,0) > 0$

(iii) $A_x[G_z(L) - g] - L$ is strictly decreasing in L

(iv) $H_y[C_u(p,w,L) + g] - L$ is strictly decreasing in L.

Condition (iii) imposes that effective excess demand for labour under demand rationing should be a decreasing function. The same property is required for supply rationing in (iv). The analogues of both conditions were derived directly from the microeconomic data for the prototype model of chapter 3. Applying the technique used in Böhm (1982), one obtains the following result.

Theorem 4.1

Assume that for all $(p,w) \gg 0$ the functions A_x, C_u, G_z, H_y are continuous and satisfy A2. Then, for every $(p,w) \gg 0$, there exists a unique allocation (L, X), which is a continuous function of the defining data (p,w) and $(M,g,\tau,\omega_0,m_0,\Pi)$.

As a consequence of this theorem one obtains again a function which determines the level of employment for all possible prices and wages. Figure 4.3 gives a schematic characterization indicating one possible partition of the price–wage space into the four disequilibrium regions and the isoemployment curves. Classical unemployment will again prevail at low prices but high wages, implying a low notional level of activity for the firm. It should be noted, however, that a constant real wage does not imply in general that employment is constant under classical unemployment. Although an equi-proportionate price and wage change implies an equal proportional change of marginal cost, the price change induces an impact through expectations on future prices which may turn the marginal rate of substitution between money and future output in either direction. Hence, a change of employment in either direction is possible. Keynesian unemployment states prevail at high wages and higher prices than classical states which cause notional excess supply on the commodity market and thus supply rationing. For a precise description of the location of all four regions (their respective boundaries) more specific assumptions on individual behaviour are required. The essential

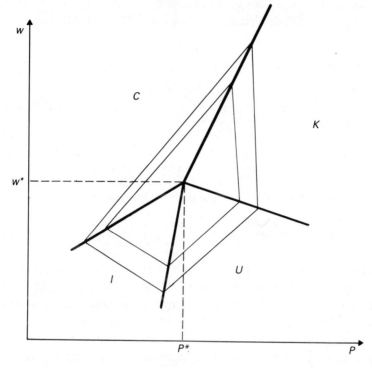

Figure 4.3

feature of the extended model with inventories, i.e. the two-sided spillover effects generated across the two markets by both groups of agents, will typically generate the four different rationing states. At the moment, no results are available which may make the description as concrete as in the simpler case without inventories. Too little is known about the role of expectations on the behavioural functions of the firm. The following analysis of the Keynesian unemployment situation for a particular expectation and objective function brings out some of the qualitative changes under alternative assumptions.

Keynesian Unemployment

The maximization problem (4.2) for the firm under a sales constraint and involuntary inventories can be written as

$$\max_{\omega} V(\omega,x) - C(\omega,\omega_0 - x) + p\omega_0 + m_0 - \Pi \qquad (4.4)$$

where $C(\omega,\omega_0 - x)$ is the restricted cost function with inventory $i = \omega_0 - x$. The first-order condition for an interior solution yields

$$V_\omega(\omega,x) = C_\omega(\omega,\omega_0 - x), \qquad (4.5)$$

i.e. marginal expected utility equals marginal cost. A marginal increase in current sales then implies a change in planned output equal to

$$\frac{\partial\omega}{\partial x} = \frac{V_{\omega x} + C_{\omega i}}{-V_{\omega\omega} + C_{\omega\omega}} = \frac{F_z^2 V_{\omega x} + V_\omega(F_i F_{zz} - F_z F_{zi})}{-(F_z^2 V_{\omega\omega} + V_\omega F_{zz})} \qquad (4.6)$$

and a change of effective labour demand equal to

$$\frac{\partial H_y}{\partial x} = \frac{\partial\omega/\partial x + F_i}{F_z} = \frac{-V_\omega F_{zi} + F_z(V_{\omega x} - F_i V_{\omega\omega})}{-(F_z^2 V_{\omega\omega} + V_\omega F_{zz})} \qquad (4.7)$$

where $V_{\omega x}$ and $V_{\omega\omega}$ denote the respective second partial derivatives of the objective function V. Clearly, the sign of (4.7), i.e. the slope of the firm's effective labour demand, plays a crucial role for the government multiplier in the Keynesian case.

Two features are immediately apparent from these equations. The effect on planned output is determined by the difference in the changes of marginal future utility and of marginal cost. Since future output constitutes an investment decision, its future return against its current costs, i.e. its profitability, determines the sign of (4.6). The role of the profitability of the investment will become even more obvious in the example below. The second important feature to notice is that the output effect must be negative and the labour demand effect will be small or even negative if a change in current rationing has no effect on future expectations. In this case $V_{\omega x} = 0$ implies that (4.6) is negative since $C_{\omega i} < 0$ under assumption F2.

Let $\psi(p)$ be the expected commodity price and assume that the firm maximizes expected total wealth. Then an optimal decision of the firm consists in choosing a production plan ω, i.e. an investment decision such that $E[\psi(p)\omega - C(\omega,\omega_0 - x)]$ is maximal. In order to develop an understanding of the role of future sales expectations on current firm behaviour, let us proceed in several steps starting from the simple case and moving to the more complicated case.

Suppose that, given the current sales constraint, the firm's future sale's constraint expectation is deterministic and assumed to be not binding. Then the necessary condition for the firm's optimal decision is given by

$$\psi(p)F_z(\omega_0 - x, z) = w$$

which yields for the slope of effective labour demand

$$\frac{\partial H_y}{\partial x} = \frac{dz}{dy} = \frac{F_{iz}}{F_{zz}} \,. \tag{4.8}$$

Equation (4.8) shows that the slope of the effective labour demand function is exclusively determined by properties of the production function. If one defines inventories and labour as complements (substitutes) if $F_{iz} < 0$ ($F_{iz} > 0$), then the effective labour demand has the 'normal' positive slope if inputs are complements and a negative slope if inputs are substitutes. If storage and new production are separable ($F_{iz} = 0$), then current changes of sales rationing have no influence on labour demand. Hence, substitutes and separability imply a decrease in output, i.e. current sales improvements reduce the profitability of real investment versus financial investment.

If expectations on future sales are such that there is a binding sales constraint $\bar{\omega}$ with probability one, then at the margin the profitability of investment must be positive, i.e.

$$\psi(p) > C_\omega(\bar{\omega}, \omega_0 - x).$$

If $\bar{\omega}$ is independent of x, any small relaxation of the current sales constraint implies that the firm takes the same investment decision $\bar{\omega}$ and substitutes labour for the reduced inventory $i = \omega_0 - x$. Hence, effective labour demand increases with a relaxation of the current sales constraint. If $\bar{\omega}$ is an increasing function of the current rationing level x the same result holds true. The positive sign of the labour demand effect can only be reversed if $\bar{\omega}$ is sufficiently decreasing in x, i.e. if current sales improvements are assumed to imply a decrease in future sales.

The two previous situations assume that future rationing occurred with either probability one or probability zero. Consider now the intermediate case where there exists some positive probability for either event and assume that the firm's expectation of the sales constraint $\tilde{y}$ in the future depends on the observed sales constraint x in the current period. More specifically, let $f(x,\tilde{y})$ denote the continuous density function of the distribution of the future sales constraints $\tilde{y}$ given x. Then, the objective function $V(\omega,x)$ of the firm takes the form

$$V(\omega,x) = \psi(p) \int \min\{\omega,\tilde{y}\} f(x,\tilde{y}) \, d\tilde{y}$$

$$= \psi(p) \left\{ \int_0^\omega \tilde{y} f(x,\tilde{y}) \, d\tilde{y} + \omega[1 - P(\omega,x)] \right\}.$$

Here P is the distribution function associated with f, i.e. $P(\omega,x)$ is the probability that the future constraint will be at most equal to ω. Thus, $1 - P(\omega,x)$ is the probability that the firm will not be sales rationed in the next period if it wanted to sell ω. The necessary condition (4.5) is

$$\psi(p)[1 - P(\omega,x)] = C_\omega(\omega,\omega_0 - x),$$

i.e. the firm chooses an investment decision whose marginal profitability is equal to zero. The impacts of a change in current rationing on planned output (4.6) and on effective labour demand (4.7) then become

$$\frac{\partial \omega}{\partial x} = \frac{-\psi(p)P_x + C_{\omega i}}{\psi(p)P_\omega + C_{\omega\omega}} \tag{4.9}$$

and

$$\frac{\partial H_y}{\partial x} = \frac{\partial \omega/\partial x + F_i}{F_z} = \frac{F_z(F_iP_\omega - P_x) - F_{iz}[1 - P(\omega,x)]}{-F_{zz}[1 - P(\omega,x)] + P_\omega F_z^2}. \tag{4.10}$$

P_x and P_ω denote the respective partial derivatives of the probability function $P(\omega,x)$. Since $P_\omega \geq 0$, $C_{\omega\omega} > 0$ and $F_{zz} < 0$, the denominator of both expressions is positive, so that their signs are those of the numerators. Therefore, the sign and size of $C_{\omega i}$, F_{iz} and P_x play the crucial role in determining the behaviour of the firm, $P_x(\omega,x)$ being the change in the probability of being rationed in the future when trying to sell ω.

In order to discuss the impact of the expectations of the firm on Keynesian equilibria, let us consider three possible cases. In the first case we assume that $P_x = P_\omega = 0$. Such a situation arises in particular if $P(\omega,x) = 0$, i.e. if the expectations are such that, in spite of the current rationing, the output decision is small enough that any future rationing level $\tilde{y}$ is larger than

ω with probability one and therefore not binding. The firm thus considers the current rationing a temporary phenomenon which will not persist in the future. The property $P_x = P_\omega = 0$ also corresponds, of course, to the case of a fixed discrete probability distribution over future possible rationing states. Equations (4.9) and (4.10) imply immediately that

$$\frac{\partial \omega}{\partial x} \lesseqgtr -F_i \quad \text{and} \quad \frac{\partial H_y}{\partial x} \lesseqgtr 0 \quad \text{iff } F_{zi} \gtreqless 0. (4.11)$$

Hence, under independent or neutral expectations concerning future rationing the slope of the firm's effective labour demand function is exclusively determined by whether inventory and labour are complements or substitutes in production. Separability of inventory holding and new production evidently determine the zero benchmark for the firm's behaviour. For the substitutes case the firm's effective labour demand is a downward-sloping function implying a decrease in planned output and in labour demand if rationing in the current period is relaxed. Such behaviour implies that the firm increases its money holdings by more than the additional revenue, i.e. at the margin the profitability of investment is less than unity, so that additional money holdings are preferable. However, comparing the levels of investment and money balances the firm plans larger output and lower money balances under sales rationing than in the notional case. Hence, a phenomenon of over-investment (i.e. excess capacity and excess inventories) and a depletion of liquidity prevails.

As an immediate consequence one obtains that the government employment multiplier

$$\frac{\mathrm{d}L}{\mathrm{d}g} = \frac{-\partial H_y/\partial x}{(\partial H_y/\partial x)(\partial C_u/\partial L) - 1} \tag{4.12}$$

is negative in the substitutes case. This somewhat striking result is exclusively due to the firm's neutral expectations that any change of the current rationing situation will have no influence on its future sales possibilities. Figure 4.4 describes the situation in the space of employment L and total sales Y. Since the graph of the effective labour demand function H_y has a negative slope, an increase in government demand from g_0 to g_1 produces a decrease in employment from L_0 to L_1.

The second case which also yields a negative government

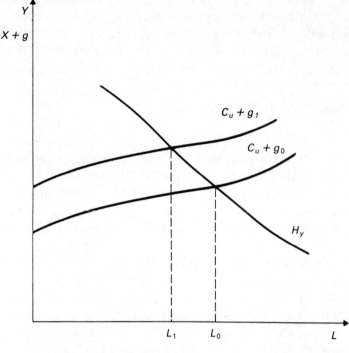

Figure 4.4

multiplier is a certain situation of pessimistic expectation, i.e.
where a current improvement is assumed to imply a sizeable
deterioration in the future. Let $P_x > 0$, i.e. the probability
$P(\omega,x)$ of being rationed in the future increases, and assume that
$P_x \geqslant P_\omega F_i$. Hence, at the margin the expected deterioration
when planning to sell the same output ω is worse than the change
if the firm tried to increase output through additional involuntary
inventory. It follows from (4.10) that the above condition implies
that $\partial H_y / \partial x$ as well as the government multiplier are negative in
the substitutes case. Hence rigid and strong pessimistic expectations make government demand policy ineffective or detrimental.

The third case to consider is when $P_x < 0$ and $P_\omega > 0$, i.e.
when expectations are such that an improvement in the current
period implies an improvement in the future. From (4.9)
it is clear that $P_x < 0$ is a necessary condition for an increase
in the profitability of investment in the substitutes case. Hence,
a large enough positive expectations effect creates a positive
investment effect and a positive labour demand effect. However,

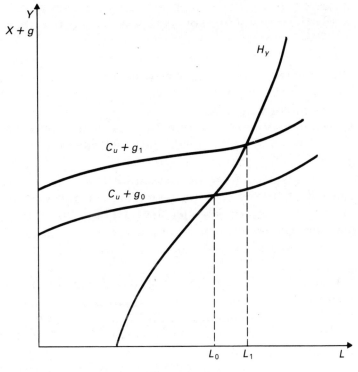

Figure 4.5

as (4.12) indicates, effective labour demand should not be too flexible with respect to changes in the sales constraint, since $(\partial H_y/\partial x)\,(\partial C_u/\partial L) > 1$ again implies a negative government multiplier. A sufficient condition to avoid this situation is that

$$-P_x \leqslant P_\omega \left[\frac{P}{\psi(p)} - F_i \right] \qquad (4.13)$$

if at the same time the marginal propensity to consume is less than unity. Relation (4.13) essentially implies that only a part of the additional sales revenue is spent for additional labour input while the other part is kept to increase money holdings. Therefore, (4.13) makes money a normal good under the sales constraint. It is straightforward to show that this implies that $\partial H_y/\partial x < p/w$. Hence, the government multiplier is positive. Figure 4.5 gives a geometric characterization in (L,Y)-space of the 'normal' situation of a positive government multiplier for the Keynesian unemployment case. If an increase in government purchases, i.e. $g_1 > g_0$, is to imply an increase in employment, i.e. $L_1 > L_0$, then the graph of H_y must be steeper than that of C_u.

Neary and Stiglitz (1983) seem to be the only economists who have investigated in a systematic way the role of expectations in a model with rationing under Keynesian unemployment. Apart from some minor modelling differences they consider exclusively the special case of binding future rationing with probability one with the assumption that inventories and labour are complements. One of their major results displays a bootstrapping effect of Keynesian expectations, i.e. pessimistic expectations increase the chances of current Keynesian equilibria. It remains an open and interesting question whether this phenomenon remains true for the more general structure presented here.

The discussion of inventory holding of the firm in this section has revealed two important qualitative differences of the extended model compared with the standard model before. The first consists of the fact that removing the asymmetry between households and firms implies a fully symmetric model with respect to the type of disequilibrium situations. Supply and demand rationing situations of both sectors appear in the short run depending on the general price–wage situation in the economy. The two situations of unemployment (classical and Keynesian) in the model have their respective counterparts of overemployment (inflationary and underconsumption) when firms would like to hire more labour. The analysis indicated that the techniques used in describing the equilibria with rationing are amenable for discussing successfully questions of short-run government policies under all four disequilibrium regimes.

The second important difference was demonstrated by taking the case of Keynesian unemployment as an example. It was shown that the success of government demand policy depends crucially on the expectations held by firms. If these were neutral or pessimistic in the sense made precise, such policy was shown to be ineffective or detrimental. As a consequence, a governmental policy directed toward the improvement of employment might have to consider other means. One such possibility may be a change of firms' expectations, a proposition as old as Keynesian analysis itself. In the framework of this model this would amount to policy measures which exert a positive influence not on the demand side but on the supply side. Thus the present model seems to be rich enough to allow an analysis of many of the issues of the current macroeconomic policy debate as well.

4.2   Money, Bonds and Credit

The most important difference between any Keynesian macro-economic model, including that presented in section 3.1 and the models described thereafter, is the absence of a market for some interest-bearing asset which enables consumers to hold wealth and transfer purchasing power from one period to the next in some form different from just holding money. Thus, all aggregate functions of the microeconomic model were independent of the price for such assets or, equivalently, of the interest rate. Similarly, investment demand by the firm in the traditional macro-economic model is associated with a demand for credit to finance expenses which generate an expected future revenue stream. The absence of such possibilities implies that there is no dependence of the aggregate functions on a possible interest rate to be paid for obtaining credit. Both aspects have been treated in different ways in the temporary equilibrium literature. The first complete treatment in a non-market clearing model was provided by Eichberger (1984a). The introduction of bonds and/or credit implies not only that, in general, the current demand and supply functions depend on one or several interest rates, but, at the same time, that the sequential structure of payments, its institutional embedding into a banking sector and the expectations of all agents involved have an impact on the nature of short-run allocations and on the effectiveness of government policies.

The introduction of bonds and of credit, however, yields two distinct structural differences for an extension of the model of section 3.2 which imply quite different results for the policy effects. Whereas the possibility of an alternative form of holding (positive) wealth through bonds for consumers induces an effect of the interest rate on the demand side for commodities, credit as a form of negative wealth has an impact on the supply side for commodities and/or on labour demand if the firm has to finance some of its purchases using credit. As a consequence, even under similar situations, policy measures by the government will create different effects on employment, output and on the interest rate. Therefore, an analysis which treats bonds and credit at the same time may embody a mixture of two opposing effects and thus not reveal the real cause for the success or failure of a particular government policy. In order to demonstrate the two distinct effects, the remainder of this section presents two separate extensions of the model of section 3.2, one with bonds only and the other with credit only.

Money and Bonds

The traditional macroeconomic literature lists two reasons for holding money, namely the transaction motive and the speculative motive. The necessity to hold money for transactions purposes arises in an intertemporal framework if the flow of expenditures and income is not perfectly synchronized in the sense that desired expenditures have to be made before an appropriate amount of income is available. If there is no credit, then agents, in general, will decide to store parts of the previous (current) income in the form of money in order to finance current (future) purchases. The source of such a desynchronized flow of revenues and outlays must be a restriction on payments that does not allow a simultaneous balancing of revenues from sales and expenditures for purchases in the same period where all payments have to be made in money. The explicit treatment of such restrictions was introduced first by Clower (1967) who suggested that an appropriate modelling corresponds to an additional constraint for each agent's budget set, allowing him to use only a fraction or nothing of current receipts for current purchases. This has been termed a Clower constraint in the temporary equilibrium literature. It has been called a cash in advance constraint by macroeconomists in the recent past (see for example Lucas, 1980). The introduction of such a constraint induces primarily a demand for credit if such a possibility exists, with only secondary effects on the demand for other assets. This feature will be exploited in the second part of this section.

The speculative motive for holding money as used in the standard macroeconomic model cannot be dissociated from the existence of an additional financial asset which an agent can use to transfer wealth from the current to a future period. In particular, such an asset must yield a greater expected return than money if a demand for the asset is to be non-zero. This implies immediately that expectations of the agents about future capital gains or losses enter into the decision-making. It is the existence of such intertemporal expectations which induces a demand for money and for other assets, and not an institutional payments restriction which forces agents to maintain money balances to secure payments.

It is a standard result from portfolio theory that an agent will hold simultaneously a (speculative) positive amount of money and of some other interest-bearing asset only if his subjective expectations on the return of the asset is sufficiently uncertain and if he is sufficiently risk averse. Moreover, the expected return on the asset must be larger than the sure return on money. In all other cases, in particular if the asset has a sure and positive return which is larger than that on money, the agent will never hold a mixed portfolio. Exploiting these general features the extension of the previous model will be based on an appropriate description of agents' expectations and preferences.

Assume that the government issues bonds which are traded in each period t on the associated bond market at the price $q_t \geqslant 0$. For any bond held over from one period to the next the government pays a fixed nominal dividend $d > 0$. Thus the total dividend payment by the government in period t is equal to dB_t, where B_t is the number of outstanding bonds held by consumers at the beginning of period t. Bonds are re-traded in each period primarily between young and old consumers. The government's intervention on the bond market to change the number of outstanding bonds corresponds to the standard open-market operation which constitutes the tool for a monetary policy.

Owing to the overlapping generations structure of consumers, old consumers in period t hold a total wealth $M_t + (q_t + d)B_t$ which they spend completely on consumption, thus supplying the number of bonds B_t on the bond market. Young consumers (i.e. workers and shareholders) have to decide on their respective demands for money and for bonds given their preferences, their budget constraints and their expectations.

Assume that price expectations are as before. The expectations concerning the future bond price are described by a density function $f(q_t,q_{t+1})$ such that $\int q_{t+1} f(q_t,q_{t+1}) dq_{t+1} = q_t$ for all q_t, i.e. the individually expected value of the future bond price is equal to the current value. Hence the young consumers view the possible fluctuations of the future bond price basically in a stationary stochastic way around the current bond price q_t with zero mean.

As a consequence the expected return on bonds is

$$Er = \frac{Eq_{t+1} + d - q_t}{q_t} = \frac{d}{q_t}$$

which is positive and a decreasing function of the current bond price for a fixed positive dividend payment d. Since the return on money is zero the assumption on expectations implies that the bond demand of a risk-averse agent will be positive for all values of q_t. Moreover, bonds dominate money for low bond prices, and the demand for bonds will tend to zero as the bond price tends to infinity since the expected rate of return tends to zero. As a consequence for any positive bond supply there always exists a market clearing bond price.

It is clear from the above discussion that for the model with instantaneous production the introduction of bonds changes only the consumer side of the economy, creating an additional dependence of consumption demand and of labour supply on the current bond price. If one follows the Keynesian assumption that the bond market always clears, then no new rationing situation for consumers will occur. Therefore, there will be the same three types of equilibria with rationing as in section 3.2. Apart from the appearance of additional spillover effects into the bond market, a detailed analysis of the model will essentially generate the same structure with the occurrence of Keynesian and classical unemployment and of repressed inflation depending on prices, wages and the other parameters given in any particular period. Thus, a complete analysis could be carried out to distinguish the effects of all government policies under the three possible regimes.

Monetary Policy and Keynesian Unemployment

The major additional feature of the extended model consists of an independent open-market policy by the government whose effectiveness will be discussed for the situation of Keynesian unemployment. This approach has to be distinguished from the monetary policy discussed in the standard Keynesian model. From the discussion of the government budget constraint in section 3.1, it is clear that, with the highly aggregated public sector (government plus central bank) discussed here, money financing or bond financing of deficits amount to opposite sides of the same coin in the short run. Nevertheless it seems much more appropriate to consider bonds (i.e. public debt), rather than the quantity of money, as the government control variable. This leaves in fact three markets (goods, labour and bonds) for which an institutional arrangement of exchange is conceptually meaningful. There is no equivalent notion of a market for money in such a model where exchange takes place. The concepts of supply and demand and of equilibrium, therefore, are much less convincing in the 'market' for money than in the other three markets. If one accepts this point of view then it becomes natural to consider the supply of bonds (more precisely the change of the stock of bonds outstanding) as the government's policy variable with the price of bonds as the market clearing device. Under this perspective changes in the amount of private money holdings have to be considered as an outcome in each feasible state rather than a policy target. This is the only acceptable view for the model without bonds and has considerable consequences for the dynamic behaviour of such models. These are analysed in chapter 5.

Given prices and wages and an employment level $L < \ell^*$ for the worker, his effective consumption demand and effective bond demand with unemployment can be written as functions of employment L and the bond price q:

$$x_w = c_u^w(q,L) \qquad b_w = b_u^w(q,L).$$

For the young shareholder, the two demand functions are his unconstrained demands given his profit income which depends on L:

$$x_s = c^s\{q, (1-\tau)[pF(L) - wL]\}$$

$$b_s = b^s\{q,(1-\tau)[pF(L) - wL]\}.$$

Let M_t and B_t denote the amounts of money and bonds respectively held by old consumers at the beginning of period t. Then aggregate private effective consumption demand and bond demand are defined as

$$C_u(q,L,M_t,B_t) = \frac{M_t + (q + d)B_t}{p}$$
$$+ c_u^w(q,L) + c^s\{q,(1-\tau)[pF(L) - wL]\}$$

$$B_u(q,L) = b_u^w(q,L) + b^s\{q,(1-\tau)[pF(L) - wL]\}.$$

Because of the overlapping generations structure one observes again that consumption demand is determined to a large extent by wealth whereas the demand for assets is independent of wealth.

A Keynesian unemployment situation is a pair (q, L) such that the commodity and the bond market clear, i.e.

(i) $C_u(q,L,M_t,B_t) + g - F(L) = 0$

(ii) $B_u(q,L) - (B_t + \Delta B) = 0$

(iii) $L < \min\{\ell^*, z^*\}$.

The two equations (i) and (ii) describing the market clearing conditions for the commodity and for the bond market are completely analogous to the corresponding conditions of the IS–LM framework. Equation (i) corresponds to the IS curve, since d/q is the nominal interest rate. Equation (ii) is the appropriate analogue of the LM curve for the bond market. Hence, there exists an equivalent geometric representation in the space of employment L and the bond price q. In order to guarantee uniqueness of the Keynesian equilibrium let us assume that for both young consumers the marginal propensities to spend on commodities, money and bonds are positive and less than unity and that consumption and money demand do not decrease when the bond price increases. This implies in particular that the demand for bonds responds negatively to an increase in the bond price with an elasticity greater than or equal to one in absolute value. Then it is straightforward to show that the two equations have the representation given in figure 4.6 if ΔB is small. $\tilde{C}$ denotes the commodity clearing locus (i) and $\tilde{B}$ denotes the bond market clearing locus (ii). The intersection $(\bar{L}, \bar{q})$ of the two curves is the Keynesian equilibrium.

From (i) and (ii) it is clear that an expansionary government demand policy implies a displacement of $\tilde{C}$ to the right; thus the government employment multiplier is positive. However, because of the positive slope of the bond market curve, this implies an increase in the bond price, i.e. a decrease in the interest rate. Conversely, an expansionary open-market operation once and for all (i.e. $\Delta B < 0$) implies an upward displacement of $\tilde{B}$, which also yields a positive employment effect in the current period. However, for any subsequent period $\Delta B < 0$ implies a negative

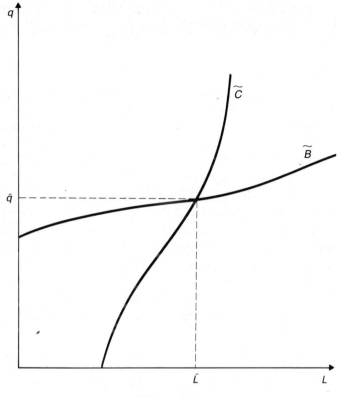

Figure 4.6

wealth effect on consumption demand, displacing the commodity market clearing locus $\widetilde{C}$ to the left. Hence, part of the positive short-run employment effect will be offset by the subsequent wealth effect. Thus, a once and for all change in the level of government debt implies an endogenous adjustment process of money holdings which in turn has implications for the level of employment, taxes, the interest rate and the government deficit. The issue is essentially the question of the long-run effectiveness of monetary policy. An answer to this question requires a systematic analysis of the government budget constraint which will be carried out in chapter 5. The particular issue of the effects of monetary policy in the long run is re-examined in section 5.3.

Transactions Constraints and Credit

At the beginning of this section it was argued that a transactions demand for money appears in a natural way if the payment structure in any time period does not allow agents to use incoming receipts from sales for expenses in the same period. In such a case current expenses have to be covered by money balances accumulated from past sales. Clower (1967), treating this problem for the first time explicitly, indicated that an institutional arrangement which requires that all payments be made using money is inconsistent with the usual one-period budget constraint used for all private agents. Hence, the introduction of a transactions constraint in any period must alter the behaviour of agents in the labour and the commodity market. Therefore, apart from providing a formalization for the well-known transactions demand for money in a choice theoretic framework of intertemporal decisions of agents, the imposition of transactions restrictions may change the qualitative properties of the temporary equilibrium allocations and may have an impact on the effectiveness of government policies.

Considering the extreme form of a transaction restriction which allows purchases only with money held over from the previous period, this would imply that a (young) consumer without any money balances has zero consumption in the first period of his life and that the demand for labour by a producer must be zero if his money balances are zero. Moreover, the demand for money held by any agent will be equal to his planned purchases in the next period. Thus, the demand for money will depend primarily on price expectations for the future. Conversely, it is clear that no new qualitative properties of the model will appear if such severe transactions restrictions are introduced on all private agents with no additional feature of the model. For example, private effective consumption demand would be independent of employment and exclusively determined by the initial wealth. However, introducing a demand for money by producers with an instantaneous production function would imply a trivial choice theoretic problem. As a consequence unemployment equilibria would appear as trivial cases with zero spillover effects in the short run and a zero government multiplier.

In a more general setting there may exist other sources to acquire funds to cover purchases such as, for example, the sale of some liquid assets. Conversely, there may be the possibility of reducing a tight transactions constraint to one allowing agents to use some proportion of their incoming receipts to be used for purchases in the same period. Another alternative would be to allow agents to obtain credit in one period to be paid back at the beginning of the next period. All these variants would eliminate the boundary cases of zero purchases if agents have zero money holdings at the beginning of a period, a situation which may occur quite frequently if there is rationing and if there are no bequests. Moreover, the trivial cases of unemployment situations disappear as soon as private agents have some possibility of influencing their current spending by current actions which induce current spill-over effects under rationing.

The work by Eichberger (1983a, b, 1984a, 1986) presents the first attempt at a systematic analysis of transactions constraints combined with a credit market in a temporary equilibrium model with quantity constraints. Observing that the possibility of obtaining credit modifies an otherwise tight transactions constraint, the demand for credit to be paid back at a later date implies an investment decision of a different kind than the portfolio problem discussed previously. Thus, in particular, a firm financing current labour purchases and retained sales (i.e. inventories) through credit makes the demand for money and the demand for labour a decreasing function of the interest rate. Hence, at first sight, it is unclear whether an expansionary government demand policy increases the interest rate and therefore decreases effective labour demand by the firm. In addition to this indirect effect via the interest rate, there may exist a crowding out effect on the credit market if, owing to the additional government expenditure, available credit to the firm decreases. Eichberger shows among other things that under a tight credit control of the banking sector an expansionary government demand policy may imply a negative government multiplier. A straightforward extension of the standard model of section 3.2, constituting a special case of Eichberger's model, will be used here to demonstrate the two effects for a Keynesian unemployment situation.

Consider an economy with a consumption sector as in section 3.2, i.e. consumers do not face a transactions constraint. In contrast, let the firm be described as in section 4.1 with inventory holding and assume that current purchases of the firm have to be financed by accumulated net wealth (i.e. initial money holdings $m_0 \geq 0$ minus profit payments $\Pi \geq 0$ minus repayments of old credit $b_0 \geq 0$) plus new credit $b \geq 0$. Thus, current receipts from sales are only available at the end of the period to be transferred to the next in the form of money.

Assume that the central bank issues a one-period credit to the firm at a nominal interest rate $r > 0$ such that interest payments have to be made in the current period. Hence, a credit of size $b > 0$ to be paid back in the next period yields a disposable liquidity in the current period of qb where $0 < q \leqslant 1$ and $1 + r = 1/q$. It is convenient here to use the variable q rather than the interest rate, bearing in mind that q and r are inversely related to each other.

Given the credit possibilities of the firm the optimization problem (4.2) under a supply constraint x becomes

$$\max V(\omega,x) + m - b \text{ subject to}$$
$$\omega = F(z,\omega_0 - y) \, ; \, \omega_0 - y \geqslant \omega_0 - x$$
$$m = py + (m_0 - \Pi - b_0 + qb - wz)$$
$$wz \leqslant m_0 - \Pi - b_0 + qb. \tag{4.14}$$

It is straightforward to show that the firm will never demand credit in excess of its immediate needs for labour purchases as long as $0 \leqslant q < 1$. Hence, for an optimal solution with $b > 0$ the last inequality of the above maximization problem is binding. In this case $m = py$. For the analysis which follows it will be assumed that the firm is able to repay its old debt and that it does not face a binding credit constraint in the current period. In fact, the formulation given in (4.14) allows the firm to repay old debt with new credit, and so the bankruptcy case does not arise. With these considerations in mind (4.14) can be written as

$$\max_{\omega} V(\omega,x) - \frac{1}{q} C(\omega,\omega_0 - x) + px$$
$$+ \frac{1}{q} [p(\omega_0 - x) + m_0 - b_0 - \Pi]. \tag{4.15}$$

As the necessary condition for an interior solution one obtains

$$qV_\omega(\omega,x) = C_\omega(\omega,\omega_0 - x) \tag{4.16}$$

which determines the effective labour demand function $H_y(q,x)$ and the effective credit demand function $B_y(q,x)$. Because of the binding inequality in (4.14) these satisfy the identity

$$qB_y(q,x) + m_0 - \Pi - b_0 = wH_y(q,x). \tag{4.17}$$

Since marginal costs are equal to w/F_z, (4.16) yields for the firm's response to a change in the interest rate

$$\frac{\partial H_y}{\partial q} = \frac{V_\omega F_z}{-q(V_{\omega\omega}F_z^2 + V_\omega F_{zz})} > 0, \tag{4.18}$$

i.e. the firm's labour demand increases with a decrease in the interest rate. As financing becomes less expensive the firm will increase its investment in future output. Together with (4.17) one has

$$q\frac{\partial B_y}{\partial q} = w\frac{\partial H_y}{\partial q} - b \tag{4.19}$$

which indicates that the firm's demand for credit may be an increasing or decreasing function of the interest rate.

Variations in the sales constraints yield the following relationships:

$$\frac{\partial \omega}{\partial x} = \frac{qV_{\omega x} + C_{\omega i}}{-qV_{\omega\omega} + C_{\omega\omega}} = \frac{F_z^2 V_{\omega x} + V_\omega(F_i F_{zz} - F_z F_{zi})}{-(F_z^2 V_{\omega\omega} + V_\omega F_{zz})} \tag{4.20}$$

$$\frac{\partial H_y}{\partial x} = \frac{-V_\omega F_{zi} + F_z(V_{\omega\omega}F_i - V_{\omega x})}{-(F_z^2 V_{\omega\omega} + V_\omega F_{zz})} \tag{4.21}$$

$$\frac{\partial B_y}{\partial x} = \frac{w}{q}\frac{\partial H_y}{\partial x}. \tag{4.22}$$

A comparison with the corresponding results of section 4.1 with inventories and no transactions constraints indicates that the effects on output and labour demand are identical. This feature was almost fully apparent from the first-order condition (4.16) which is identical with (4.5) except that the interest rate enters in a multiplicative way. Hence, one finds that the qualitative behaviour of the firm for each given interest rate $1/q$ is the same as in the model without transactions constraints and without credit. Therefore the firm's behaviour with respect to changes in current rationing depends primarily on its expectations about future rationing and its technology for any current interest rate. It is immediate, then, that a negative government multiplier may occur for the same reason as in section 4.1.

In order to demonstrate that the interest rate effect and a crowding out effect alone may reverse the sign of government demand multiplier, let us assume that credit demand behaves normally, i.e.

$$\frac{\partial B_y}{\partial q} > 0, \tag{4.23}$$

and that expectations on future rationing are sufficiently optimistic so that $\partial H_y/\partial x > 0$. Furthermore, assume that the central bank pursues a credit policy which restricts total private credit to a fixed nominal supply $\bar{B} > 0$ and that the interest rate always adjusts in such a way that effective credit demand is equal to the supply $\bar{B}$. Then, a Keynesian unemployment situation is defined by a triple (q, L, Y) such that

$$
\begin{aligned}
&\text{(i)} & C_u(L) + g &- Y = 0 \\
&\text{(ii)} & B_y(q, Y) &- \bar{B} = 0 \\
&\text{(iii)} & H_y(q, Y) &- L = 0
\end{aligned}
\tag{4.24}
$$

Differentiating (4.24) with respect to g yields the three multipliers

$$\frac{dL}{dg} = \frac{\dfrac{\partial H_y}{\partial x}\bar{B}}{-\left(\dfrac{\partial C_u}{\partial L}\dfrac{\partial H_y}{\partial x}\bar{B} + q\dfrac{\partial B_y}{\partial q}\right)} \tag{4.25}$$

$$\frac{dq}{dg} = \frac{q\dfrac{\partial B_y}{\partial x}}{-\left(\dfrac{\partial C_u}{\partial L}\dfrac{\partial H_y}{\partial x}\bar{B} + q\dfrac{\partial B_y}{\partial q}\right)} \tag{4.26}$$

$$\frac{dY}{dg} = \frac{q\dfrac{\partial B_y}{\partial q}}{\dfrac{\partial C_u}{\partial L}\dfrac{\partial H_y}{\partial x}\bar{B} + q\dfrac{\partial B_y}{\partial q}}. \tag{4.27}$$

The last expression is positive but less than unity, implying that sales increase by less than the government demand increases. The other two multipliers are negative, so that employment falls and the interest rate rises. Thus, increased government demand induces a higher interest rate which reduces the profitability of investment. Under the tight credit constraint this effect is sufficiently strong to reduce employment. It is straightforward to see that these effects will be reinforced if the amount of credit $\bar{B}$ available for the firm is reduced because of the expansion of government demand. In such a case a true crowding out on the market for credit would occur.

It is instructive to consider the system (4.24) in a reduced form. The tight credit constraint of equation (ii) which is maintained under the change of government purchases imposes a monotonic relationship between the interest rate and sales. Thus, (ii) and (iii) together yield a modified effective labour demand function $\widetilde{H}_y$ taking the market clearing condition (ii) into account. Therefore, differentiating (ii) and (iii) yields

$$\frac{\partial \widetilde{H}_y}{\partial x} = - \frac{\bar{B}\,(\partial H_y/\partial x)}{\partial B_y/\partial q} \tag{4.28}$$

which is negative because of (4.23). Rewriting (4.24) as

$$\begin{aligned}
\underset{\sim}{C}_u\,(L) + g - Y &= 0 \\
H_y\,(Y) - L &= 0
\end{aligned} \tag{4.29}$$

yields the multiplier (4.25) as

$$\frac{dL}{dg} = \frac{\partial \widetilde{H}_y/\partial x}{1 - (\partial \widetilde{H}_y/\partial x)\,(\partial C_u/\partial L)}. \tag{4.30}$$

Figure 4.7 provides a geometric characterization of (4.29) in the usual quantity space. Owing to the negative slope of $\widetilde{H}$ one observes that employment falls from L_0 to L_1 because of the increase in government demand from g_0 to g_1. A decrease of $\bar{B}$ in credit available to the private sector due to an additional government demand in that market implies a displacement of $\widetilde{H}$ to the left, thus creating an even stronger negative effect on employment.

The results of this section indicated that the speculative motive and the transactions motive to hold money imply quite different roles of the interest rate. For the speculative motive, i.e. for the positive wealth-holding aspect with bonds as an alternative to money, standard methods of portfolio theory were used to confirm the traditional Keynesian result about the effectiveness of open-market operations in the short run. However, in the long run (see section 5.3), the policy effects are reversed. The number of outstanding government bonds is positively correlated with

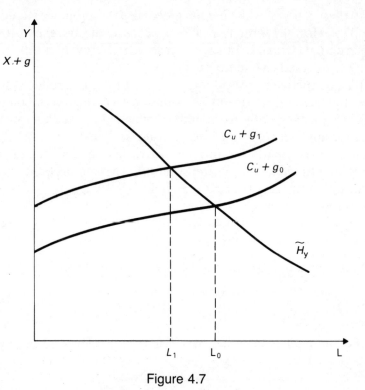

Figure 4.7

long-run stationary employment levels. In either case, bonds as
an alternative to money imply a modification of the aggregate
commodity demand function with no essential qualitative changes
for the model if firms hold inventories and are allowed to hold a
mixed portfolio as well. However, transactions restrictions with
the possibility of credit for firms imply an interest rate effect on
effective labour demand. Combined with a constant credit constraint of the banking sector, the firms' effective labour demand
function under supply rationing becomes a downward-sloping
function if the interest rate effect is taken into account. In this
case, the government employment multiplier is negative with a
reinforcement of this effect if there is additional crowding out.
Hence, an expansionary government demand policy without a
simultaneous expansion of private credit possibilities has a negative effect on employment, constituting a second source for the
failure of fiscal policy in addition to the expectations effect of the
previous section.

5

The Dynamics of Temporary Equilibria with Quantity Rationing

The preceding chapters provided an extensive description and analysis of an ongoing economy at an arbitrarily chosen point of time t. For that particular period the past history of the economy was given and its influence on the particular time period consisted primarily in fixed values of the stock variables money, bonds and inventories. Moreover, prices of commodities and the wage rate were assumed to be given and in general to be non-Walrasian, implying that transactions had to be carried out under non-market clearing conditions. A systematic description of the evolution of such temporary equilibria with quantity rationing requires that both elements of the dynamic process, namely the adjustment mechanism of prices and wages and the change in the stock variables, which are basically the outcome of the decisions of the agents and of the quantity constraints, are analysed simultaneously.

The literature contains very little in terms of a systematic theory of how prices and wages ought to change if a rationing situation occurs in a particular time period. Two approaches, however, can be distinguished. The first adheres to the basic idea underlying a perfectly competitive adjustment process. Taking some definition of effective excess demand, its sign determines the direction of price and wage change. This may be called a modified version of the law of supply and demand. Applying this adjustment process raises again the issue of which is the appropriate concept of effective demand, as was discussed in detail in chapter 2. The second approach departs from the purely competitive adjustment process by imposing monopolistic and/or other institutional rules, e.g. wage indexation, real wage targets and others. Such contributions represent attempts to remodel downward wage rigidities or the Phillips curve phenomenon. Most of these adjustment rules, however, are formulated more or less in an *ad hoc* way without establishing some underlying generally applicable principle.

For either approach, interesting insights from a macroeconomic point of view can only be expected if both driving forces in a temporary equilibrium context, i.e. the stock adjustment as well as the price and wage dynamics, are investigated simultaneously. Some of the interesting questions to be asked are the following.

1 What are the properties of a reasonable price and wage adjustment rule under quantity rationing?
2 Which are the steady states of such a rule and what are their determining factors?
3 Which equilibria are stable or unstable?
4 Is the medium-run and/or long-run behaviour of the economy cyclical? Does it exhibit regime switching?
5 What is the role of agents' expectations?

The following analysis attempts to give some answers to these questions. Although the structure of an overlapping generations model possesses all the necessary ingredients for a systematic investigation of all five questions, question (3) will not be treated at all, and only some structural implications for (4) will be indicated. The published work of market clearing models dealing with stability and cyclicity gives ample evidence of the complexity and of the difficulties involved. With quantity rationing the degree of complexity clearly does not decrease. Section 5.1 provides the general dynamic structure of the prototype model. A complete description of the set of perfect foresight steady states is given in section 5.2. Section 5.3 analyses employment and welfare for alternative steady states. A general class of price and wage adjustment rules within the competitive spirit is described in 5.4 and its steady states are characterized in section 5.5. Some results on extensions of the prototype model are given in section 5.6.

5.1 Money, Prices and Wages

Consider the prototype economy described in section 3.2. For the dynamic development of such an economy, assume that economic activity starts at $t = 1$ at which some old generation of consumers is endowed with an initial quantity of money $M_1 > 0$. Then sequences of temporary equilibria with quantity rationing can be defined in a straightforward way. Given the stationary structure of the economy (a stationary population, no technical change), the analysis of chapter 3 implies that there is a time-invariant allocation rule $\mathcal{L}$ which determines the level of employment and the type of rationing situation for arbitrary prices, wages and money holdings in each period, given a government policy and agents' expectations. Making all these elements explicit, the employment function is given by

$$L_t = \mathcal{L}(p_t, w_t, M_t, p^w_{t+1}, p^s_{t+1}, g, \tau). \tag{5.1}$$

Since $\mathcal{L}$ is homogeneous of degree zero in its first five arguments, one can write (5.1) as

$$L_t = \mathcal{L}(\alpha_t, m_t, \theta^w_t, \theta^s_t, g, \tau) \tag{5.2}$$

where $\alpha_t = w_t/p_t$ is the real wage, $m_t = M_t/p_t$ are real money balances and $\theta^w_t = p^w_{t+1}/p_t$ and $\theta^s_t = p^s_{t+1}/p_t$ are the expected rates of price increase (one plus the inflation rate) by both consumers. For a given government policy (g, τ) and fixed expected inflation rates (θ^w_t, θ^s_t), the function $\mathcal{L}$ as given in (5.2) determines a partition of the space of real money holdings and of the real wage into the three regimes C, K and I. The characterization of the partition given in figure 5.1 assumes given expected inflation rates (θ^w, θ^s) and that labour supply is monotonically increasing in the real wage in addition to assumptions C1, C2 and F1.

In chapter 3 it was indicated that for the exogenous government real demand g and the proportional tax rate τ, government deficits and thus net savings by consumers are determined endogenously. Therefore, final money holdings in each period depend on the level of employment and on the rationing situation. Hence, some care has to be taken concerning the adjustment of the stock of money, since demand rationing of old consumers and/or the government cannot be excluded for arbitrary prices and wages. Let (L_t, x^w_t, x^s_t) denote the allocation for young consumers in period t for given (M_t, p_t, w_t). Then final money holdings M_{t+1} equal nominal savings by the young. However, feasibility and the demand rationing rule introduced in chapter 3 imply that

$$x^w_t + x^s_t = \max\{0, F(L_t) - g - M_t/p_t\}.$$

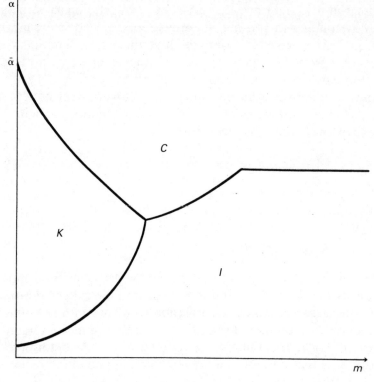

Figure 5.1

Therefore,

$$M_{t+1} = p_t \min\{ F(L_t), g + M_t/p_t\} - \tau[p_t F(L_t) - w_t L_t] \quad (5.3)$$

which yields the money adjustment equation in real variables as

$$m_{t+1} \, \theta_t = \min\{ m_t + g, F(L_t)\} - \tau[F(L_t) - \alpha_t L_t]. \quad (5.4)$$

Both equations correspond to the usual government budget constraint if output is at least as large as real balances plus government demand. If output is smaller, then young agents are demand rationed to zero, so that all their net income is saved. Equation (5.3) and therefore (5.4) assume implicitly that any excess real balances of old consumers under demand rationing is destroyed or confiscated by the government and not transferred to the young generation.

Finally, the expectation formation of young consumers has to be described in more detail for the full dynamic analysis than in the temporary case. Again it is assumed that all generations use the same expectation function. As is customary in overlapping generations models agents make a point forecast for p^i_{t+1} ($i = w, s$) on the basis of current and past prices over a finite number of periods. For the purposes here, the following form of the expectation function is convenient:

$$p^i_{t+1} = p_t \psi^i \left(\frac{p_t}{p_{t-1}}, \frac{p_{t-1}}{p_{t-2}}, \ldots, \frac{p_{t-T}}{p_{t-(T+1)}} \right) \qquad i = w, s \quad (5.5)$$

or written more compactly

$$\theta^i_t = \psi^i \left(\theta_{t-1}, \ldots, \theta_{t-T} \right) \qquad\qquad i = w, s. \quad (5.6)$$

ψ^i describes consumer i's forecast of the inflation rate based on past actual inflation rates. It will be assumed that ψ^i is continuous and that past observations of identical inflation rates imply the same forecast, i.e. $\theta = \psi^i (\theta, \ldots, \theta)$ holds for all $\theta > 0$ and $i = w, s$. This formulation includes many forms of adaptive expectations as well as possibilities of learning from past prices. It clearly implies perfect foresight under constant inflation.

The three equations (5.1), (5.3) and (5.5) or (5.2), (5.4) and (5.6) describe the full dynamic framework of the prototype model. Formally a sequence $\{\alpha_t, m_t, \theta_t\}^\infty_{t=1}$ is called an equilibrium with quantity rationing if

(i) $m_{t+1} \theta_t = \min\{m_t + g, F(L_t)\} - \tau [F(L_t) - \alpha_t L_t]$

(ii) $L_t = \mathscr{L}(\alpha_t, m_t, \theta^w_t, \theta^w_t, g, \tau)$ $\qquad\qquad\qquad\qquad$ (5.7)

(iii) $\theta^i_t = \psi^i (\theta_{t-1}, \ldots, \theta_{t-T})$ $\qquad i = w, s.$

This formulation does not specify any particular price and wage adjustment, i.e. $\{\alpha_t, \theta_t\}^\infty_{t=1}$ can take any form at the moment.

5.2   Quasi-stationary Equilibria and Perfect Foresight

Perfect foresight equilibria with quantity rationing are obtained in the same fashion as in the standard market clearing models by the fact that price expectations coincide with actual prices. Here this means that $\theta^i_t = \theta_t$ for all t, which makes condition (iii) in (5.7) redundant. Hence a sequence $\{\alpha_t, m_t, \theta_t\}^\infty_{t=1}$ is an equilibrium with quantity rationing and perfect foresight if

$$m_{t+1} \, \theta_t = \min\{m_t + g, F(L_t)\} - \tau \, [F(L_t) - \alpha_t \, L_t]$$
$$L_t = \mathscr{L}(\alpha_t, m_t, \theta_t, g, \tau). \tag{5.8}$$

It is not immediately apparent from this definition whether it is justified to call a sequence generated by (5.8) an equilibrium with perfect foresight in prices *and* quantity constraints. States with rationing of young consumers alone, whether on the labour market or on the commodity market, cause no difficulty since the behaviour of young agents is defined assuming no future rationing. In general, expected future demand rationing creates spillover effects into the current period on the commodity market and on the labour market. These are ignored in (5.8) so that, strictly speaking, it describes perfect foresight equilibria with rationing of young agents alone, each of them assuming that future constraints are not binding. If these were binding the function $\mathscr{L}$ would have to depend on m_{t+1} which implies, in principle, the possibility of three distinct additional rationing situations. The hierarchy of the demand rationing mechanism, which excludes old consumer rationing before young consumers are rationed to zero, eliminates two of them, namely classical and inflationary states with no young consumer rationing. However, old consumer rationing in Keynesian states violates the one-sidedness rule of a D-equilibrium. Still, the nature of the inflationary states will differ when effective labour supply of young workers depends on future demand rationing. If this occurs then labour supply and employment will be less under such expectations than without them.

In the case of a fixed labour supply the problem associated with non-zero spillovers from future rationing on current labour supply does not arise. Moreover, in all inflationary states the employment level is constant and young consumer demand rationing implies that future expected rationing has no spillover effect on current demand, so that sequences of inflationary states are perfect foresight even under old consumer rationing. Current consumption is best against the future rationing constraint given the constant current real income. The only issue remaining involves situations when regime switching occurs from Keynesian states to inflationary states with old consumer rationing. Whether these are possible under (5.8) and fixed labour supply is unclear. Since the main objective of this section is to describe the steady states with perfect foresight the switching problem can be neglected. In order to avoid the spillover effects of future rationing on labour supply the description of the steady states will be carried out for the case of a fixed labour supply.

Associated with an equilibrium with quantity rationing $\{\alpha_t, m_t, \theta_t\}_{t=1}^{\infty}$ is its allocation $\{L_t, x_t^w, x_t^s, X_t^0\}_{t=1}^{\infty}$ of employment and of consumption of young and old consumers. Candidates for long-run steady states are those equilibria which induce constant allocations. It is straightforward to see that such an allocation obtains if and only if the real wage and real money holdings are constant over time. Therefore, an equilibrium is called *quasi-stationary* if $\alpha_t = \alpha_{t'}$, $m_t = m_{t'}$ and $\theta_t = \theta_{t'}$, for all t and t'. It is called *stationary* if in addition $\theta_t = 1$ for all t which implies $p_t = p_{t'}$, $w_t = w_{t'}$ and $M_t = M_{t'}$ for all t and t'. Hence, in a quasi-stationary equilibrium all nominal entities grow or decrease at the same constant rate, while at a stationary equilibrium nominal as well as real quantities are constant through time. Formally, a quasi-stationary equilibrium with perfect foresight and quantity rationing (given fixed labour supply) is a triple $(\alpha, m, \theta) \gg 0$ such that

$$m(\theta - 1) = g - \tau[F(L) - \alpha L] \\ + \min\{0, F(L) - g - m\} \tag{5.9}$$

$$L = \mathscr{L}(\alpha, m, \theta, g, \tau).$$

Before proceeding to the general description and characterization of the quasi-stationary equilibria, the market clearing situation will be analysed separately. Two existence theorems are provided, one for the general case of flexible labour supply and one for the case of fixed labour supply. In the second case a generic condition for uniqueness is given as well.

With the notation of chapter 3 notional excess demands on both markets can be written as functions of $(\alpha_t, m_t, \theta_t)$ in each period. Then a sequence $\{\alpha_t, m_t, \theta_t\}_{t=1}^{\infty}$ is a Walrasian equilibrium with perfect foresight if, for all $t = 1, \ldots,$

$$D(\alpha_t, m_t, \theta_t) = m_t + c^w(\theta_t, \alpha_t) + c^s[\theta_t, (1 - \tau)\Pi(1, \alpha_t)] \\ + g - F[h(\alpha_t)] = 0$$

$$Z(\alpha_t, \theta_t) = h(\alpha_t) - a(\theta_t, \alpha_t) = 0 \tag{5.10}$$

$$m_{t+1}\theta_t = m_t + g - \tau\Pi(1, \alpha)$$

hold. (α, m, θ) is quasi-stationary if

$$F[h(\alpha)] = m + c^w(\theta, \alpha) + c^s[\theta, (1 - \tau)\Pi(1, \alpha)] + g$$

$$h(\alpha) = a(\theta, \alpha) \tag{5.11}$$

$$m \, (\theta - 1) = g - \tau \Pi \, (1, \, \alpha)$$

or equivalently $(\alpha, \, \theta)$ is quasi-stationary if

(i) $\dfrac{1}{\theta} \, \{F \, [h \, (\alpha)] - c^{w} \, (\theta, \, \alpha) - c^{s} \, [\theta, \, (1 - \tau) \, \Pi \, (1, \, \alpha)] - \tau \Pi \, (1, \, \alpha)\}$

$+ \, c^{w} \, (\theta, \, \alpha) + c^{s} \, [\theta, \, (1 - \tau) \, \Pi \, (1, \, \alpha)] + g - F \, [h \, (\alpha)] = 0$

$$(5.12)$$

(ii) $h \, (\alpha) - a \, (\theta, \, \alpha) = 0.$

The existence of such an equilibrium is essentially guaranteed under the assumptions C1, C2 and F1 provided that government demand is not too large. It is straightforward to see that labour market clearing implies a largest positive lower bound $\underline{\alpha}$ for the equilibrium real wage which determines a maximum feasible output of $F \, [h \, (\underline{\alpha})]$. Clearly, if $g \geq F \, [h \, (\underline{\alpha})]$, then no equilibrium exists. However, $g < F \, [h \, (\underline{\alpha})]$ is not a sufficient condition in general, since aggregate private consumption cannot be made arbitrarily small unless some additional assumptions are imposed on consumer preferences. Theorems 5.1 and 5.2 provide two alternatives. Theorem 5.2 implies in particular that inflationary equilibria will occur if g is sufficiently large within the given bounds.

Theorem 5.1

Assume C1–C3 and F1 and define

$$\underline{\alpha} = \inf\{\alpha \mid h \, (\alpha) - a \, (\theta, \, \alpha) = 0, \, \theta > 0\}.$$

For every $\varepsilon > 0$ and $g \leq \tau \Pi \, (1, \, \underline{\alpha}) - \varepsilon$ there exists a quasi-stationary Walrasian equilibrium.

Proof   C1–C3 and F1 imply the existence of a continuous and decreasing function $\mu \, (\theta) = \alpha$ such that for every $\theta > 0$

$$h \, [\mu \, (\theta)] - a \, [\theta, \, \mu \, (\theta)] = 0.$$

Define the excess demand function on the commodity market under labour market clearing as

$$D \, (\theta) = m \, (\theta) + c^{w} \, [\theta, \, \mu \, (\theta)] + c^{s} \, \{\theta, \, (1 - \tau) \, \Pi \, [1, \, \mu \, (\theta)]\}$$
$$+ \, g - F \, \{h \, [\mu \, (\theta)]\}$$

where

$$m(\theta) = \frac{1}{\theta}\Big\{F\{h[\mu(\theta)]\} - c^w[\theta, \mu(\theta)]$$

$$- c^s\{\theta, (1-\tau)\Pi[1, \mu(\theta)]\} - \tau\Pi[1, \mu(\theta)]\Big\}.$$

C1, C2 and F1 imply $D(\theta) > 0$ for θ small since $m(\theta) \to \infty$ as $\theta \to 0$ and $\mu(\theta) \geqslant \underline{\alpha} > 0$. However, $\theta > 1$ implies

$$D(\theta) < g - \tau\Pi[1, \mu(\theta)]$$

$$\leqslant \tau\Pi(1, \underline{\alpha}) - \varepsilon - \tau\Pi[1, \mu(\theta)].$$

Hence, $D(\theta)$ is less than zero for θ sufficiently large since $\mu(\theta) \to \underline{\alpha}$ as $\theta \to \infty$. Therefore, the intermediate value theorem yields the result.

QED

The uniqueness of quasi-stationary equilibria is a much more delicate problem. Judging from the results of Grandmont (1983) and others one may expect that there always coexist two types of equilibria, namely one with $\theta^* = 1$ and some other with $\theta^{**} \neq 1$. This seems to be a feature of the pure exchange case which does not prevail in the prototype model in general. The source of this difference lies in the fact that there is production and possibilities for a non-balanced budget of the government. Still, fairly strong additional assumptions are required for uniqueness.

Theorem 5.2

Assume C1, C2, F1 and $v' = 0$ and let α^* be the unique market clearing real wage for the labour market. Define aggregate private demand under quasi-stationarity and full employment $\bar{L}$ as

$$X(\theta, \tau) = \frac{1}{\theta}\Big\{F[h(\alpha^*)] - \tau\Pi(1, \alpha^*)\Big\}$$

$$+ \Big(1 - \frac{1}{\theta}\Big)\Big\{c^w(\theta, \alpha^*\bar{L})$$

$$+ c^s[\theta, (1-\tau)\Pi(1, \alpha^*)]\Big\}.$$

Let

$$X(\tau) = \inf\{X(\theta, \tau) \mid \theta > 0\}$$

and

$$\varepsilon\,(\tau) = \; F\,[h\,(\alpha^*)] - \tau\Pi\,(1,\,\alpha^*) - X\,(\tau) > 0.$$

(i) There exists a quasi-stationary Walrasian equilibrium if and only if
$$g \leqslant \tau\Pi\,(1,\,\alpha^*) + \varepsilon\,(\tau).$$

(ii) The Walrasian equilibrium is unique for all $(g,\,\tau)$ with $g \leqslant \tau\Pi\,(1,\,\alpha^*) + \varepsilon\,(\tau)$ if and only if $X\,(\theta,\,\tau)$ is decreasing in θ.

At first sight the assumption that aggregate demand is decreasing in θ may seem very strong. However, under C1 and C2 this property always holds for $\theta < 1$ and in a neighbourhood of $\theta = 1$. For $\theta > 1$ it rules out strong substitution effects for both consumers. It holds, for example, if marginal propensities to consume are constant or if the elasticity of substitution is not too far above unity. Geometrically speaking the condition implies for each consumer that its offer curve should have a slope steeper than minus one if its slope is negative. Statement (ii) not only provides a sufficient condition for uniqueness for a particular government policy. It implies that the monotonicity of aggregate demand is a necessary and sufficient condition for uniqueness for all policies $(g,\,\tau)$ for which Walrasian equilibria exist. Therefore, uniqueness and monotonicity imply each other.

Proof Aggregate excess demand is given by

$$D\,(\theta) = X\,(\theta,\,\tau) + g - F\,[h\,(\alpha^*)]$$

which is positive for θ small. Therefore, $D\,(\theta)$ is less than or equal to zero for some θ if and only if

$$g \leqslant F\,[h\,(\alpha^*)] - \inf\,[X\,(\theta,\,\tau)]$$
$$= \cdot\tau\Pi\,(1,\,\alpha^*) + \varepsilon\,(\tau)$$

which proves (i). If $X\,(\theta,\,\tau)$ is decreasing in θ, then $D\,(\theta)$ has at most one zero. To prove the converse, suppose $X\,(\theta,\,\tau)$ is not decreasing for some τ. Then, there exist $\theta_1 > \theta_2 > 1$ such that $X\,(\theta_1,\,\tau) = X\,(\theta_2,\,\tau)$. But then, θ_1 and θ_2 are equilibria for $g = F\,[h\,(\alpha^*)] - X\,(\theta_1,\,\tau)$ which satisfies $g = F\,[h\,(\alpha^*)] - X\,(\theta_1,\,\tau) \leqslant \tau\Pi\,(1,\,\alpha^*) + \varepsilon\,(\tau)$.

QED

The two results on existence and uniqueness are in line with the intuition which governs similar results in the standard overlapping generations literature. It should be emphasized, however, that neither existence nor uniqueness are required for the subsequent analysis of quasi-stationary equilibria or for the analysis of price and wage adjustment mechanisms in the subsequent sections. However, if a Walrasian equilibrium exists it is almost never stationary with zero inflation and a balanced government budget. In general, i.e. for an arbitrary choice of a stationary government policy, given preferences and technology, a Walrasian quasi-stationary equilibrium displays either positive inflation with a permanent government deficit or negative inflation with a permanent government surplus. This is most evident for the case with a fixed labour supply. The labour market clearing real wage then uniquely defines real profits in equilibrium which are equal to the ratio of g/τ only by accident. The relationship of the ratio g/τ to real profits in Walrasian equilibrium, or equivalently the size of real government demand to real taxes, also plays a decisive role in determining the type of quasi-stationary equilibrium under the class of price and wage adjustment mechanisms discussed below.

Returning to the general case of system (5.8), the assumption of theorem 5.2 will be maintained for the remaining discussion of quasi-stationary equilibria. In this case the employment function $\mathscr{L}$ possesses some clear and important properties which are easily derived. First, states of repressed inflation occur only for real wages α less than α^*, the labour market clearing real wage. However, classical states require a real wage α greater than α^*. For given $\theta > 0$, the function $\mathscr{L}$ has the typical representation given in figure 5.2. As usual the isoemployment curves are added. The line connecting the points $(m, \alpha) = (F(\bar{L}) - g, 0)$ and $(m, \alpha) = (0, \bar{\alpha})$ separates states with old consumer rationing (above and to the right) from those without (below and to the left). The downward-sloping boundary $K \cap I$ is determined by a marginal propensity to consume of workers which is larger than that of shareholders. The same property holds for the slope of the isoemployment curves in states with Keynesian unemployment. This confirms the feature of a positive real wage multiplier. For the other Keynesian multipliers one finds

$$\frac{\partial \mathscr{L}}{\partial m} = \frac{\partial \mathscr{L}}{\partial g} > 0$$

and

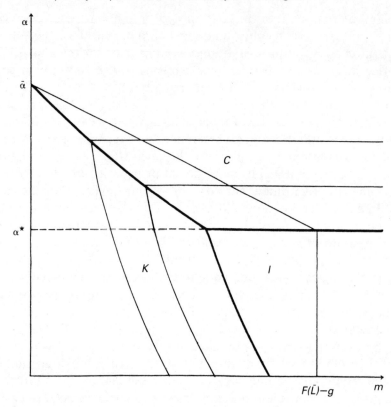

Figure 5.2

$$\frac{\partial \mathscr{L}}{\partial \theta} = \left(\frac{\partial c^w}{\partial \theta} + \frac{\partial c^s}{\partial \theta} \right) \frac{\partial \mathscr{L}}{\partial m}$$

whose sign is not unambiguous.

The analysis of the quasi-stationary equilibria now leads to theorem 5.3 given below. It establishes that for every $(\theta, \alpha) \gg 0$ there exists $m > 0$ such that (α, m, θ) is quasi-stationary. Hence long-run steady states may occur for any positive real wage and any rate of price change whether positive, zero or negative. Therefore, no element of the model, in particular not even the choice of a specific government policy· (g, τ), restricts a priori the set of perfect foresight steady states. The theorem also indicates that uniqueness of quasi-stationary equilibria always obtains under inflation, i.e. for all (θ, α) with $\theta > 1$ or if the governments share in maximal output $g/F(\bar{L})$ is larger than or equal to the tax rate τ. If this last condition is not satisfied there always exists a continuum of (θ, α) with $\theta < 1$ for which multiple equilibria arise.

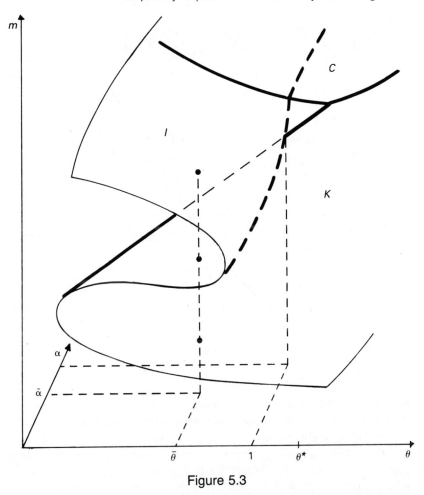

Figure 5.3

Hence, multiplicity is generic. If labour supply is not fixed, then the multiplicity also arises under inflation, whereas uniqueness is true in general if government demand is larger than the maximal amount of real taxes. Figure 5.3 illustrates the steady state manifold in (θ, α, m)-space. $(\bar{\theta}, \bar{\alpha})$ is a point for which three distinct quasi-stationary equilibria exist. All Keynesian unemployment states are located on the lower portion of the manifold. Repressed inflation states without old consumer rationing occur on the backward bend and on the upper part near the Walrasian equilibrium. All repressed inflation states on the upper portion of the manifold to the left of the heavy broken line exhibit old consumer rationing. In the diagram it is assumed that there exists a unique quasi-stationary Walrasian equilibrium $(\alpha^*, m^*, \theta^*)$

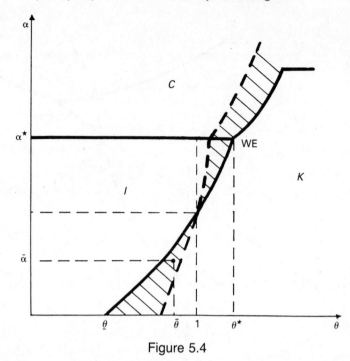

Figure 5.4

with $\theta^* > 1$, i.e. $g > \tau\Pi(1, \alpha^*)$. Figure 5.4 provides the associated two-dimensional analogue, i.e. the projection of the manifold onto (θ, α)-space. Keynesian unemployment states lie to the right of the heavy solid line $(\underline{\theta}, \text{WE})$. Repressed inflation states without old consumer rationing occur in the shaded area, and states with old consumer rationing lie to the left of the heavy broken line.

Theorem 5.3

Assume C1, C2, F1 and $v' = 0$, and denote by I_0 the set of quasi-stationary states of repressed inflation with rationing of old consumers.

(i)   For every $(\theta, \alpha) \gg 0$ such that $\theta > 1$ there exists a unique $m > 0$ such that (α, m, θ) is quasi-stationary.

(ii) If $F(\bar{L}) > g \geqslant \tau F(\bar{L})$, then for every $(\theta, \alpha) \gg 0$ there exists a unique $m > 0$ such that (α, m, θ) is quasi-stationary.

(iii) If $g < \tau F(\bar{L})$, then there exists an open set $B \subset (0, 1) \times \mathbb{R}_{++}$

such that for all $(\theta, \alpha) \in B$ there are $0 < m_1 < m_2 < m_3$ such that $(\alpha, m_i, \theta), i = 1, 2, 3$, are quasi-stationary and $(\alpha, m_1, \theta) \in K$, $(\alpha, m_2, \theta) \in I \setminus I_0$ and $(\alpha, m_3, \theta) \in I_0$.

Proof For every $(\alpha, m, \theta) \geqslant 0$ define the function

$$H(\alpha, m, \theta) = g - \tau[F(L) - \alpha L] + \min \{0, F(L) - g - m\}$$
$$L = \mathscr{L}(\alpha, m, \theta).$$

H is well defined, continuous, non-increasing in m and $H(\alpha, 0, \theta) > 0$. (α, m, θ) is quasi-stationary if and only if $(\theta - 1) m = H(\alpha, m, \theta)$.

(i)   If $\theta > 1$, then the function $H(\alpha, m, \theta) - (\theta - 1)m$ is strictly monotonically decreasing in m and tending to minus infinity for $m \to \infty$. This combined with the fact that $H(\alpha, 0, \theta) > 0$ yields the result.

(ii) Let $\theta \leqslant 1$ and $F(\bar{L}) > g \geqslant \tau F(\bar{L})$ and define the unique pair $(\tilde{m}, \tilde{L})$ by $F(\tilde{L}) = g + \tilde{m}$. For all $m > \tilde{m}$ rationing of old consumers occurs and the employment level is constant and equal to $\tilde{L} = \mathscr{L}(\theta, \alpha, m)$. Therefore, one obtains

$$H(\alpha, m, \theta) - m(\theta - 1) = \begin{cases} \begin{aligned} & g - \tau[F(L) - \alpha L] \\ & \quad + (1 - \theta)m \end{aligned} & m \leqslant \tilde{m} \\[2em] \begin{aligned} & F(\tilde{L}) - \tau[F(\tilde{L}) - \alpha \tilde{L}] \\ & \quad - \theta m \end{aligned} & m \geqslant \tilde{m} \end{cases}$$

$g \geqslant \tau F(\tilde{L})$ implies that $g - \tau[F(L) - \alpha L] > 0$ for all $\alpha > 0$ and $L = \mathscr{L}(\alpha, m, \theta)$. Hence, $H(\alpha, m, \theta) - m(\theta - 1) > 0$ for $\theta \leqslant 1$ and $m \leqslant \tilde{m}$. For $m \geqslant \tilde{m}$, the function is strictly monotonically decreasing and tending to minus infinity. The same argument as above implies the result.

(iii) Let $g < \tau F(\bar{L})$ and consider the function $H(\alpha, m, \theta)/m$. Then (α, m, θ) is quasi-stationary if and only if $H(\alpha, m, \theta)/m = \theta - 1$. In order to demonstrate the assertion it is sufficient to show that there exist $0 < \underline{m} < \bar{m}$ and $(\bar{\theta}, \bar{\alpha}) \geqslant 0$ such that

$$H(\bar{\alpha}, \underline{m}, \bar{\theta})/\underline{m} < \bar{\theta} - 1 < H(\bar{\alpha}, \bar{m}, \bar{\theta})/\bar{m}.$$

The continuity of H then implies the result. Figure 5.5 illustrates the essential argument in the proof.

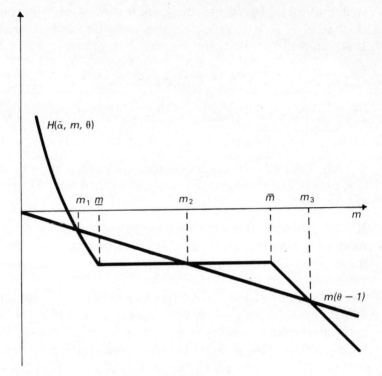

$H(\bar{\alpha}, m, \theta)$

$m_1 \underline{m}$ m_2 $\bar{m}$ m_3 m

$m(\theta - 1)$

Figure 5.5

Choose $\alpha' < \alpha^*$ with $g - \tau [F(\bar{L}) - \alpha' \bar{L}] < 0$ and let

$$\bar{\theta} - 1 = \frac{g - \tau [F(\bar{L}) - \alpha' \bar{L}]}{F(\bar{L}) - g}.$$

If $\bar{m} = F(\bar{L}) - g$, then $H(\alpha', \bar{m}, \bar{\theta})/\bar{m} = \bar{\theta} - 1$. Thus $(\alpha', \bar{m}, \bar{\theta})$ is a quasi-stationary equilibrium.

Define

$$\underline{m} = F(\bar{L}) - g - c^w(\bar{\theta}, \alpha' \bar{L}) - c^s \{\bar{\theta}, (1 - \tau) [F(\bar{L}) - \alpha' \bar{L}]\}.$$

Feasibility and C1, C2 imply that $0 < \underline{m} < \bar{m}$. Moreover,

$$\frac{H(\alpha', \underline{m} \,\bar{\theta})}{\underline{m}} < \frac{g - \tau [F(\bar{L}) - \alpha' \bar{L}]}{F(\bar{L}) - g} = \frac{H(\alpha', \bar{m}, \bar{\theta})}{\bar{m}} = \bar{\theta} - 1.$$

For small $\varepsilon > 0$ and $\bar{\alpha} = \alpha' + \varepsilon$ one obtains

$$\frac{H(\bar{\alpha}, \underline{m} \,\bar{\theta})}{\underline{m}} < \bar{\theta} - 1 = \frac{H(\alpha', \bar{m}, \bar{\theta})}{\bar{m}} < \frac{H(\bar{\alpha}', \bar{m}, \bar{\theta})}{\bar{m}}.$$

Hence, the result follows.

QED

One of the important consequences of the generic multiplicity of quasi-stationary equilibria is the fact that it may exclude monotonic dynamic behaviour globally. Hence, cycles or even chaotic behaviour are possible. If the assumption of constant labour supply is dropped, multiplicity may arise under inflation as well, thus increasing the possibilities for cycles. In general one concludes that cyclical behaviour arises typically if under constant government demand the tax revenue function generates deficit and surplus states for the same price and wage steady states, i.e. when the same real wage and the same inflation rate can be associated with different levels of economic activity and/or rationing situations.

The multiplicity result stated in theorem 5.3 is not due to the particular asymmetry of the tax scheme which taxes profits only. Rather it is a consequence of a feature alluded to in the discussion above, i.e. the fact that the governments share in maximal output $g/F(\bar{L})$ is less than the tax rate τ. This condition in general allows states with a government surplus. In the case of a proportional income tax on both consumers the same type of multiplicity of quasi-stationary states arises. The following example illustrates this.

Suppose both consumers have the same Cobb–Douglas utility function with a marginal and average propensity $0 < c < 1$ to consume out of income. In this case aggregate consumption when young is independent of the real wage and of expected inflation. Given real money holdings $m > 0$ of old consumers and the proportional tax rate $0 < \tau < 1$ on income, a Keynesian unemployment situation is simply a solution L of

$$F(L) - g = m + (1 - \tau) c F(L)$$
$$L < \bar{L}, F'(L) > \alpha. \tag{5.13}$$

Quasi-stationarity implies that

$$m = \frac{1}{\theta}\left[(1 - \tau)(1 - c) F(L)\right]$$

so that Keynesian quasi-stationary equilibria are given as solutions (θ, L) of

$$F(L) \{1 - (1 - \tau) [c + (1 - c)/\theta]\} = g. \tag{5.14}$$

If $g < \tau F(\bar{L})$, then the Walrasian rate θ^* of price increase is given by

$$\theta^* = \frac{(1 - \tau)(1 - c)}{1 - c(1 - \tau) - g/F(\bar{L})} \tag{5.15}$$

which is less than unity. Assume that $\theta^* < 1 - \tau$ which is equivalent to $g/F(\bar{L}) < c\tau$. In this case it is straightforward to calculate that for every θ with $\theta^* < \theta < 1 - \tau$ and $\alpha < \alpha^*$ there exist three distinct quasi-stationary equilibria (α, m_1, θ), (α, m_2, θ) and (α, m_3, θ) with

$$m_1 = \frac{g - \tau F(L)}{\theta - 1} \qquad L < \bar{L}$$

$$m_2 = \frac{g - F(\bar{L})}{\theta - 1}$$

$$m_3 = \frac{(1 - \tau) F(\bar{L})}{\theta}$$

such that $(\alpha, m_1, \theta) \in K$, $(\alpha, m_2, \theta) \in I \backslash I_0$ and $(\alpha, m_3, \theta) \in I_0$. In addition, a similar multiplicity arises for some $\alpha > \alpha^*$, i.e. for (θ, α) there exist states which are Keynesian, classical without old consumer rationing and classical with old consumer rationing. Figure 5.6 provides an illustration of the result. Keynesian states are to the right of the solid line. The shaded area contains consumer demand rationing states which are inflationary for $\alpha < \alpha^*$ and classical for $\alpha > \alpha^*$. States with old consumer rationing are to the left of the heavy broken line.

5.3   Employment and Welfare in the Long Run

The results of the previous section show that the possibility of non-Walrasian allocations in an overlapping generations model adds an additional degree of indeterminacy of equilibria. This is not present in macroeconomic models within the same general structure which treat market clearing situations only. In essence, the requirement of perfect foresight and of a long-run constant allocation imposes no restriction whatsoever on the type of dis-

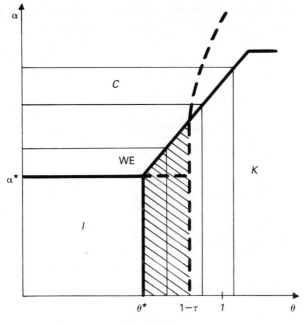

Figure 5.6

equilibrium situation or on the level of employment. This also leaves real wages, inflation rates and government policy variables to be determined. The latter are considered truly exogenous, so that their influence on the steady states is of interest. The simple stationary structure of the policy chosen here actually suffices to capture most long-run consequences of government influences, since non-stationary policies are not consistent in general with steady states. It should be kept in mind, however, that in contrast with most overlapping generations models with government activity in the literature, all monetary or real transfers are excluded here. Taxes are not lump sum, so that deficits and the process of money creation are completely endogenous. This makes a comparison of the features of the two models even more difficult, since non-market clearing situations already distort any direct comparison.

Examination of the impact of changes of exogenous parameters on the steady state variables of an economy is sometimes called a comparative dynamics analysis as opposed to comparative statics. This amounts to a comparison of different constant but infinite sequences of variables for two different economies with the same time horizon but different constant levels of some of the parameters for all time periods. Clearly such an analysis cannot describe the effects of a once and for all change of one of the parameters at some finite date. With these restrictions for the interpretation of the results, theorem 5.3 can now serve as a basis for a systematic analysis of the long run, i.e. the steady state effects of policy measures on the level of employment and on welfare. The most interesting cases to be discussed here are Keynesian quasi-stationary equilibria with positive inflation. According to the theorem, $\theta > 1$ implies a unique equilibrium (α,m,θ) for every $\alpha > 0$. Let (α,m,θ) be a Keynesian unemployment quasi-stationary equilibrium. Then (α,m,θ) solves

$$m(\theta - 1) = g - \tau[F(L) - \alpha L]$$
$$L = \mathscr{L}(\alpha,m,\theta,g,\tau).$$

Hence, there exists a steady state employment function $L = \bar{\mathscr{L}}(\alpha,\theta,g,\tau)$ which is defined by the unique solution of

$$L = \mathscr{L}\left(\alpha, \frac{g - \tau[F(L) - \alpha L]}{\theta - 1}, \theta, g, \tau\right). \tag{5.16}$$

Let

$$\Delta = \frac{\partial \mathscr{L}}{\partial m} \frac{\tau(F' - \alpha)}{\theta - 1}$$

which is positive. Then the long-run government demand multiplier is

$$\frac{\partial \bar{\mathscr{L}}}{\partial g} = \frac{1}{1 + \Delta}\left(\frac{\partial \bar{\mathscr{L}}}{\partial g} + \frac{1}{\theta - 1}\frac{\partial \mathscr{L}}{\partial m}\right)$$

$$\tag{5.17}$$

$$= \frac{1}{1 + \Delta} \frac{\theta}{\theta - 1} \frac{\partial \mathscr{L}}{\partial g}.$$

Therefore, under positive inflation quasi-stationary Keynesian unemployment equilibria with higher government demand have higher levels of employment, which confirms the long-run effectiveness of government demand policy. Since the real wage and the inflation rate are kept constant, this implies a smaller real deficit and smaller real balances. Next consider a comparison of alternative tax rates. As the tax multiplier one obtains

$$\frac{\partial \overline{\mathscr{L}}}{\partial \tau} = -\frac{F(L) - \alpha L}{1 + \Delta} \left(\frac{\partial c^s}{\partial \Pi} + \frac{1}{\theta - 1} \right) \frac{\partial \mathscr{L}}{\partial m} \tag{5.18}$$

which is negative. Hence, lower tax rates are associated with higher levels of employment, and therefore with smaller real deficits and smaller real balances. Thus, under a constant real wage and a constant positive rate of inflation, the long-run government demand and tax multipliers have the same sign as those for each temporary equilibrium.

The remaining two multipliers are those with respect to the real wage and the rate of inflation. One obtains

$$\frac{\partial \overline{\mathscr{L}}}{\partial \alpha} = \frac{\partial c^w / \partial W - (1 - \tau) \partial c^s / \partial \Pi + \tau / (\theta - 1)}{1 + \Delta} L \frac{\partial \mathscr{L}}{\partial m} \tag{5.19}$$

and

$$\frac{\partial \overline{\mathscr{L}}}{\partial \theta} = \frac{1}{1 + \Delta} \left(\frac{\partial \mathscr{L}}{\partial \theta} - \frac{m}{\theta - 1} \frac{\partial \mathscr{L}}{\partial m} \right)$$

$$\tag{5.20}$$

$$= \frac{\partial c^w / \partial \theta + \partial c^s / \partial \theta - m / (\theta - 1)}{1 + \Delta} \cdot \frac{\partial \mathscr{L}}{\partial m} .$$

The real wage multiplier is positive if the marginal propensity to consume of the worker is larger than that of the shareholder. The more interesting expression is (5.20). It is straightforward to show that the numerator of the first term is negative if and only if aggregate private demand under quasi-stationarity is a decreasing function of θ. This same condition was used in theorem 5.2 and it was equivalent to uniqueness of quasi-stationary Walrasian equilibria. Therefore, the inflation multiplier is negative if and only if Walrasian equilibria are unique for all admissible government policies. Hence, other things being equal, higher inflation in the long run means lower levels of employment. Therefore, there is a clear negative trade-off in the long run between positive inflation and employment and not the converse as might be suggested by the reasoning of the Phillips curve.

Some interesting questions arise if one considers a government demand policy with an inflation control. The two multipliers (5.17) and (5.20) describe the trade-offs for a joint policy. Figure 5.7 displays three monotonically increasing curves of constant employment, where $L_1 < L_2 < L_3$. Thus, the negative employ-

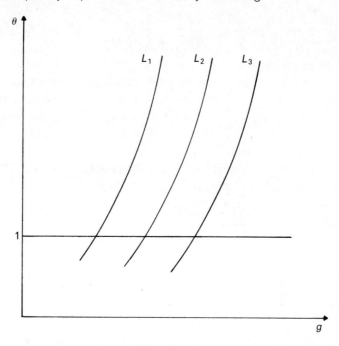

Figure 5.7

ment effect of a smaller government demand may be offset by an appropriate reduction in inflation. Conversely, a higher steady state inflation rate requires a higher government demand to maintain the same long-run level of employment.

The correct modelling of perfect foresight allows a utility comparison of alternative quasi-stationary states. It is well known from the literature of overlapping generations models that Walrasian equilibria are inefficient if and only if they are inflationary. The intuition behind this result, well understood since Samuelson's seminal contribution, is that $\theta > 1$ implies an inefficient trade-off for consumers between consumption when young and consumption when old. Essentially the same result applies here as well for inflationary unemployment equilibria. Consider a quasi-stationary Keynesian unemployment equilibrium (α,θ,g,τ) with positive inflation $(\theta > 1)$. Since there is no demand rationing the intertemporal marginal rate of substitution for both consumers is the same and equal to θ. Therefore the utility levels are given by the ordinary indirect utility functions $V^w(\theta,\alpha L)$ for the worker and by $V^s\{\theta,(1 - \tau) [F(L) - \alpha L]\}$ for the shareholder. This implies the utility changes

$$\frac{dV^w}{d\theta} = V^w_\theta + \alpha V^w_\theta \frac{\partial \overline{\mathcal{L}}}{\partial \theta} < 0$$

$$\frac{dV^s}{d\theta} = V^s_\theta + (1 - \tau)(F' - \alpha) V^s_\Pi \frac{\partial \overline{\mathcal{L}}}{\partial \theta} < 0. \tag{5.21}$$

Hence, a lower rate of inflation yields a higher steady state level of utility for both consumers. Here the Pareto improvement has two causes. The first is the direct effect of a better intertemporal rate of substitution, whereas the second supplements the first through higher production and higher incomes. Thus, reducing inflation under long-run unemployment not only increases employment in K but also improves steady state utility of both agents. If unemployment is classical the utility effect is not decisive, since employment stays constant but demand rationing changes. Roughly one finds that the utility effect is the same as above near the boundary to the Keynesian region. Summarizing these results one should consider high (positive) inflation under unemployment as a major cause for permanent welfare losses.

A change of government policy parameters under Keynesian unemployment and positive inflation implies welfare changes in the same direction as the employment changes, as one can see immediately from (5.21). Hence higher government demand and a lower tax rate both yield Pareto improvements. As a consequence there are associated welfare trade-offs between inflation and government demand for a joint parameter change similar to the employment trade-offs described above.

It is useful to derive a global representation for the utility mapping associated with the set of all quasi-stationary equilibria for a given government policy. Figure 5.8 gives a possible characterization of the quasi-stationary utility allocations. It is again assumed that $g < \tau F(\bar{L})$ and $g > \tau \Pi(1,\alpha^*)$, so that figure 5.4 corresponds to figure 5.8. Its properties are now developed in several steps, using figure 5.9 also.

Consider first allocations for (α^*,θ), $\theta < \theta^*$. All these states belong to $C \cap I$ which implies demand rationing of consumers. Since the real income of both agents stays constant, $\theta < \theta^*$ implies a demand for money which is even higher than notional demand because of the rationing on the commodity market. Since $x^w + m^w + x^s + m^s = F(\bar{L}) - g$ is constant, feasibility and the

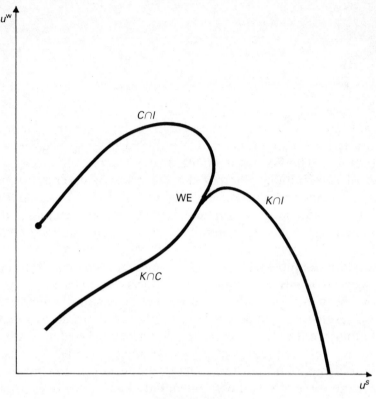

Figure 5.8

budget constraint imply that the demand rationing has to be such that there is a one-to-one exchange of current and future consumption between generations. As θ declines the consumption path of each consumer follows the thick line in figure 5.9, which represents the situation of the worker. This implies that $x^w + x^s = 0$ and $m^s + m^w = F(\bar{L}) - g$ for some θ_1 with $1 < \theta_1 < \theta^*$. Since $x^s + x^w$ declines monotonically in θ the two agents observe first increasing and then decreasing utility. For $\theta \leq \theta_1$ rationing of old consumers occurs and the allocation and therefore utility is constant for the two agents. Hence, $(\alpha^*, \theta) \in C \cap I$ generates a continuous path in utility space which is increasing first and then returns to a level below WE.

Next consider $(\alpha, \theta) \in K \cap I$ with $\alpha < \alpha^*$. Since both α and θ decline along $K \cap I$ the utility of the shareholder increases. As α tends to zero the utility of the worker must go to zero and the utility of the shareholder must be increasing. The relationship

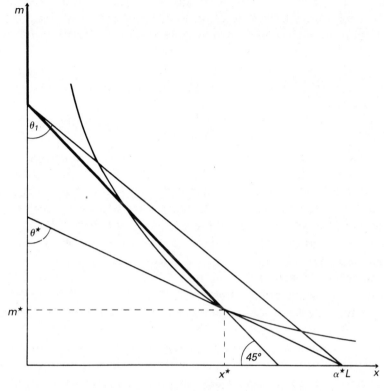

Figure 5.9

between income and the substitution effect determines whether the utility of the worker is increasing near WE or not. Finally, the boundary $C \cap K$ is mapped onto a monotonic line connecting the origin with WE. The global representation shows quite clearly that a Walrasian equilibrium with positive inflation will be Pareto dominated by equilibria with quantity rationing. This confirms again the type of results shown in different contexts by Böhm and Puhakka (1988) and Böhm and Keiding (1986).

To conclude, it must be evident now that in a stationary environment (no population growth, no capital accumulation) inflation is one of the most important causes for suboptimality. First, it drives a wedge between social and private marginal rates of substitution for any given amount of total production and government real demand. Second, high inflation yields low employment and low output. Therefore, inflation reduces welfare for two distinct reasons. To consider only the aspect of the trade-off between the consumption of young and old consumers under different rates of inflation as an indicator of welfare redistributions is an incomplete characterization, which creates the false implication in many marcoeconomic texts that no general welfare loss is involved. Positive inflation, i.e. negative real rates of interest in steady states, implies unambiguous permanent welfare losses.

5.4   The Law of Supply and Demand under Quantity Rationing

Returning to the general dynamic description of the prototype model as given by equations (5.7), a general class of price and wage mechanisms, called the law of supply and demand, will now be formulated which is built on the general competitive paradigm. This leaves aside any monopolistic elements as well as any a priori assumed rigidities whether in nominal or real terms. The basic principle of price adjustment of the competitive paradigm states that the sign of price changes, if necessary, should be the same as the sign of the associated excess demand. In spite of some well-known weakness which *tâtonnement* processes with these adjustment rules may have, the general principle is universally accepted. Its application in the case of equilibria with rationing seems equally plausible and it has been used by several economists in one way or another. The standard argument is straightforward. A market with demand (supply) rationing leaves a potential buyer (seller) unsatisfied who, in order to increase his utility, would be willing to pay more (charge less) for additional purchases (sales). Hence, prices and wages should increase under demand rationing and decrease under supply rationing. Although very acceptable at first sight such a rule possesses some drawbacks. It is essentially static and myopic and it ignores some important aspects of dynamic economies, since it sets tomorrow's prices according to today's experience. The endogenous structural changes from one period to the next may actually call for different adjustments if market clearing is the desired goal. Typically the set of rationed agents changes, or the change in money balances implies a regime switching. Market clearing today may require a price increase for tomorrow's market clearing which the rule cannot indicate. As a consequence stationary Walrasian equilibria are essentially the only market clearing situations which are generated by such a rule, and these exist under special circumstances only, as was shown above. Another important observation is that the law of supply and demand cannot incorporate any systematic effects of expectations or of past experience. These enter only through the impact of agents' expectations on the prevailing equilibrium in each period. Therefore it may not be surprising that this rule generates steady states which do not display some of the standard macroeconomic heuristic arguments: Phillips curve type reasoning, real wage negotiations among workers and firms, inflation-compensated wage increases (indexation) etc. It is an open question whether the law of supply and demand can be modified to generate these features. Some attempts in this direction are presented in a volume edited by Hénin and Michel (1982). These will be commented on and compared with the results here at the end of this section.

Some economists, most notably Hahn (1980b), support the view that 'some feature of imperfect competition is required for a coherent non-Walrasian model' and 'that in such an equilibrium prices are not fixed by fiat but are the outcome of the decisions of rational calculating agents' (p. 7). It is by no means clear whether this is a necessary condition for a coherent theory. Moreover, the absence of imperfect competition does not imply that prices have to be fixed by fiat. As the model below demonstrates, the competitive paradigm, with market forces (or an auctioneer) determining price and wage changes, provides a coherent non-Walrasian theory which may well serve as a consistent framework to analyse macroeconomic issues. This may be considered as a first step, but also as a point of reference for models of a more sophisticated nature with strategic behaviour of monopolistic agents setting prices.

A description of the law of supply and demand requires that a particular adjustment rule and a quantitative measure of disequilibrium have to be formulated for each market. Given (g, τ), suppose that the temporary situation in period t is given by $(\alpha_\tau, m_t, \theta_t^w, \theta_t^s)$ which determines uniquely employment and consumption in the associated disequilibrium state. Let $s_t^\ell \in [-1, 1]$ and $s_t^c \in [-1, 1]$ denote two associated disequilibrium measures, s_t^ℓ for the labour market and s_t^c for the commodity market. The price and wage adjustment describing the law of supply and demand will be defined by two continuous functions $p : [-1, +1] \to (-1, +\infty)$ and $w : [-1, +1] \to (-1, +\infty)$ which determine the rate of increase in prices and wages, i.e.

$$p_{t+1} = p_t[1 + p(s_t^c)]$$

$$w_{t+1} = w_t[1 + w(s_t^\ell)]. \tag{5.22}$$

The two functions p and w are assumed to be time independent. They are strictly monotonically increasing with $p(0) = 0$ and $w(0) = 0$. It should be observed that the formulation chosen here assumes that there are no adjustment effects across the two markets, i.e. the signal on each market is taken as the sole indicator for the adjustment on that market. More complex functions with non-zero cross-effects seem reasonable as well.

In chapter 2 it was indicated that there exists no direct way to derive disequilibrium measures from market signals alone in the framework of the D-equilibrium, since individual agents do not express effective desired demands and supplies which differ from actual trades. However, it is possible to construct consistent measures if one combines the effective demand and supply functions with the aggregate notional levels. An example at the end of this section will serve to illustrate a class of functions which determines the appropriate measures.

Before the general properties of the signalling functions can be described, a particular feature of the present model, which implies a discontinuity of any consistent signalling function, has to be elucidated. The basic notion associated with a pair (s^ℓ, s^c) of disequilibrium measures imposes that s^j, $j = \ell, c$, is negative under supply rationing and positive under demand rationing. Therefore $s^\ell < 0$ in the interior of $K \cup C$, $s^c < 0$ in the interior of K, $s^c > 0$ in the interior of $I \cup C$, and $s^\ell > 0$ in the interior of I. The changes of regimes from demand to supply rationing imply that $s^c = 0$ on $K \cap C$ and $s^\ell = 0$ on $C \cap I$, which is compatible with a continuous change of the measure across these two boundaries. However, for states on $K \cap I$, a continuous change of both measures would imply that $s^c = s^\ell = 0$ on $K \cap I$. This clearly contradicts the general underlying notion that all measures should be zero only if the Walrasian equilibrium has been obtained. On $K \cap I$ there is no consumer rationing, but the producer faces constraints on both markets. One of them is always redundant because of the atemporal structure of the producer model. Therefore an associated pair of disequilibrium measures should be non-zero which implies that any pair of signalling functions generating such measures cannot both be continuous on $K \cap I$. This discontinuity is exclusively due to the atemporal modelling of production. It was noticed by others as well (e.g. Ito, 1980; Honkapohja and Ito, 1981; Michel and Picard, 1982). As soon as inventory holdings were introduced, the appearance of the fourth state of underconsumption would eliminate the discontinuity problem.

Let σ^j, $j = \ell$,c, denote the signalling functions for the two markets which define for every possible state $(\alpha,m,\theta^w,\theta^s)$ the two equilibrium measures $s^\ell = \sigma^\ell(\alpha,m,\theta^w,\theta^s)$ and $s^c = \sigma^c(\alpha,m,\theta^w,\theta^s)$. Then it will be said that the signalling functions σ^j, $j = \ell$,c, are consistent if they generate disequilibrium measures (s^ℓ,s^c) which satisfy the following assumption.

Assumption P1

(i) $(\alpha,m,\theta^w,\theta^s)\ \in\ \text{int}(C \cup I)$ $\qquad \Rightarrow\ s^c > 0$
$(\alpha,m,\theta^w,\theta^s)\ \in\ \text{int}\ K$ $\qquad \Rightarrow\ s^c < 0$
$(\alpha,m,\theta^w,\theta^s)\ \in\ K \cap C$ $\qquad \Rightarrow\ s^c = 0$

(ii) $(\alpha,m,\theta^w,\theta^s)\ \in\ \text{int}(C \cup K)$ $\qquad \Rightarrow\ s^\ell < 0$
$(\alpha,m,\theta^w,\theta^s)\ \in\ \text{int}\ I$ $\qquad \Rightarrow\ s^\ell > 0$
$(\alpha,m,\theta^w,\theta^s)\ \in\ C \cap I$ $\qquad \Rightarrow\ s^\ell = 0$

(iii) $(\alpha,m,\theta^w,\theta^s)\ \in\ (K \cap I)\backslash\text{WE}$ $\qquad \Rightarrow\ s^\ell > s^c = 0.$

Conditions (i) and (ii) are the straightforward formalization of the intuitive notions described above. Condition (iii) imposes a demand rationing signal on the labour market on $K \cap I$. As a consequence σ^ℓ must have a discontinuity there. Elsewhere, σ^ℓ can be chosen to be continuous, as is σ^c over the total domain.

To conclude this section we shall give an example of a pair of consistent signalling functions satisfying assumption P1. Let $(\alpha_t,m_t,\theta^w_t,\theta^s_t)$ denote a particular state in period t and L_t and X_t its associated employment level and aggregate private consumption level respectively. Since (L_t, X_t) are uniquely associated with each disequilibrium, one can write $(L_t, X_t) \in K$ (or I, or C) whenever $(\alpha_t,m_t,\theta^w_t,\theta^s_t) \in K$ (or I, or C). Let L^*_t and X^*_t denote the notional levels of the consumption sector and Z^*_t and Y^*_t the notional levels of the producer in period t. Define

$$s^c_t = -\frac{X_t + g - Y^*_t}{Y^*_t}\frac{L_t - A_x(X_t)}{A_x(X_t)} + \frac{X^*_t - X_t}{X^*_t}\frac{C_u(L_t) - X_t}{C_u(L_t)}.$$

It is easy to verify that $s_t^c \in [-1,1]$ and that

$$(L_t, X_t) \in \text{int}(C \cup I) \qquad\qquad \Rightarrow s_t^c > 0$$
$$(L_t, X_t) \in \text{int } K \qquad\qquad \Rightarrow s_t^c < 0$$
$$(L_t, X_t) \in (K \cap C) \cup (K \cap I) \qquad \Rightarrow s_t^c = 0.$$

Moreover, s_t^c is continuous across $K \cap I$. In order to satisfy the condition $(s_t^\ell, s_t^c) \neq 0$ on $K \cap I$, s_t^ℓ will be defined in the following way:

$$s_t^\ell = -\frac{L_t - L_t^*}{L_t^*}\frac{L_t - A_x(X_t)}{A_x(X_t)} + \frac{Z_t^* - L_t}{Z_t^*}\frac{C_u(L_t) - X_t}{C_u(L_t)}$$
$$+ \frac{Z_t^* - L_t}{Z_t^*}\mathbf{1}_0\left[-\frac{L_t - L_t^*}{L_t^*}\frac{L_t - A_x(X_t)}{A_x(X_t)}\right.$$
$$\left. + \frac{Z_t - L_t}{Z_t^*}\frac{C_u(L_t) - X_t}{C_u(L_t)}\right]$$

where $\mathbf{1}_0 : \text{IR} \to \text{IR}$ denotes the function

$$\mathbf{1}_0(x) = \begin{cases} 0 & x \neq 0 \\ 1 & x = 0. \end{cases}$$

Clearly, s_t^ℓ *satisfies*

$$(L_t, X_t) \in \text{int}(C \cup K) \qquad \Rightarrow s_t^\ell < 0$$
$$(L_t, X_t) \in \text{int } I \qquad\qquad \Rightarrow s_t^\ell > 0$$
$$(L_t, X_t) \in \text{int } C \cap I \qquad \Rightarrow s_t^\ell = 0$$
$$(L_t, X_t) \in (K \cap I)\backslash\text{WE} \qquad \Rightarrow s_t^\ell > 0.$$

Moreover, s_t^ℓ is continuous except on $(K \cap I)\backslash\text{WE}$.

5.5 Quasi-stationary Equilibria and the Law of Supply and Demand

The complete dynamic system under disequilibrium price and wage adjustment combines the equations (5.7) with the price adjustment rules (5.22) and the signalling functions σ^j, $j = \ell,c$. Therefore, $\{\alpha_t, m_t, \theta_t\}_{t=1}^\infty$ is called an equilibrium with quantity rationing and consistent price adjustment or a consistent equilibrium if, for all $t = 1, \ldots$,

(i) $\theta_t = 1 + p(s_t^c)$

(ii) $\alpha_{t+1} = \alpha_t \dfrac{1 + w(s_t^\ell)}{1 + p(s_t^c)}$ \hfill (5.23)

(iii) $m_{t+1} = \dfrac{1}{\theta_t} \left\{ \min\{m_t + g, F(L_t)\} - \tau[F(L_t) - \alpha_t L_t] \right\}$

such that

(iv) $L_t = \mathscr{L}(\alpha_t, m_t, \theta_t^w, \theta_t^s)$

(v) $s_t^j = \sigma^j(\alpha_t, m_t, \theta_t^w, \theta_t^s)$ $\qquad\qquad\qquad$ j = c,ℓ

(vi) $\theta_t^i = \psi^i(\theta_{t-1}, \ldots, \theta_{t-T})$ $\qquad\qquad\qquad$ i = s,w.

A quasi-stationary consistent equilibrium is defined by a triple (α, m, θ) solving

(i) $\theta - 1 = p(s^c) = w(s^\ell)$ $\qquad\qquad\qquad\qquad\qquad$ (5.24)

(ii) $mp(s^c) = g - \tau[F(L) - \alpha L] + \min[0, F(L) - g - m]$

such that

(iii) $L = \mathscr{L}(\alpha, m, \theta, \theta)$

(iv) $s^j = \sigma^j(\alpha, m, \theta, \theta)$ $\qquad\qquad\qquad\qquad$ j = c,ℓ

(v) $\theta = \psi^i(\theta, \ldots, \theta)$ $\qquad\qquad\qquad\qquad$ i = s,w.

It follows immediately from (i) that prices and wages must move in the same direction and that the corresponding disequilibrium signals must have the same sign. This excludes any quasi-stationary state of classical unemployment, due to P1. Condition (v) indicates that quasi-stationary consistent equilibrium satisfy perfect foresight. Conditions (i), (ii) and P1 imply that price and wage changes must have the same sign as the government deficit. Hence, apart from the exceptional situation that the Walrasian equilibrium is stationary, in which case it is a stationary consistent equilibrium with a balanced government budget, the only two possibilities are consistent equilibria with long-run unemployment, permanent deflation and a government surplus, or consistent equilibria with long-run demand rationing, permanent inflation and a positive government deficit. This clearly shows that there can be no long-run Phillips curve yielding a trade-off between positive inflation and unemployment.

It is straightforward to show that a linear expectation-augmented price and wage adjustment process does not change the qualitative nature of this last result. Define a pair of expectation-augmented adjustment processes by

$$\widetilde{w}(s_t^\ell) = w(s_t^\ell) + \beta(\theta_t^e - 1)$$
$$\widetilde{p}(s_t^c) = p(s_t^c) + \beta(\theta_t^e - 1)$$

for some $0 < \beta < 1$, where θ_t^e is the commonly expected inflation rate $\theta_t^e = \theta_t^w = \theta_t^s$. Then, the conditions for quasi-stationarity are

(i) $w(s^\ell) = p(s^c)$

(ii) $m[p(s^c) + \beta(\theta^e - 1)] = g - \tau [F(L) - \alpha L]$
$+ \min\{0, F(L) - g - m\}.$

Imposing the condition $\theta = \theta^e$ of correct expectations implies

$$\theta - 1 = p(s^c) + \beta(\theta - 1)$$

or

$$(\theta - 1) (1 - \beta) = p(s^c).$$

Hence, unemployment steady states are again associated with deflation and positive inflation occurs only under demand rationing, i.e. under repressed inflation. Therefore, even an expectation-augmented law of supply and demand does not generate a long-run Phillips curve in general.

A proof of existence of quasi-stationary consistent equilibria requires two further assumptions.

Assumption P2

(α, m, θ) and (α', m', θ') with

$$L > \mathscr{L}(\alpha, m, \theta, \theta) > \mathscr{L}(\alpha', m', \theta', \theta')$$

implies

$$\sigma^\ell(\alpha, m, \theta, \theta) > \sigma^\ell (\alpha', m', \theta', \theta').$$

Assumption P2 imposes a monotonic relationship between the unemployment signal s^ℓ and the level of employment. This is a very natural assumption, since any signal which is monotonic in the unemployment rate indicates less rationing under less unemployment. The example in the preceding section satisfies P2.

Assumption P3

There exists a continuous function $a : \mathbb{R}_+^2 \rightarrow \mathbb{R}$ associating with each real money balance m and each inflation rate θ a real wage $\alpha = a(m, \theta)$ such that

(i) $w\{\sigma^\ell[a(m, \theta), m, \theta, \theta]\} = p\{\sigma^c[a(m, \theta), m, \theta, \theta]\}$

(ii) $a(m,\theta) > 0$ if $(m,\theta) \gg 0$.

At first sight this assumption seems unnecessarily strong. It imposes joint restrictions on the price and wage adjustment functions and on the signalling functions. However, it is actually fairly weak and allows a large class of adjustment and signalling functions. Again, because of the atemporal structure of the producer model, continuity of the adjustment and signalling functions (except on $K \cap I$) alone cannot exclude the situation where the real wage falls under all Keynesian states and under all states of repressed inflation. Either case would exclude the existence of quasi-stationary consistent equilibria. This problem is related to the degenerate boundary $K \cap I$ and it disappears as soon as inventory holding is allowed. Then, in most cases, continuity of the adjustment and signalling functions would suffice to show existence.

Theorem 5.4

Assume that $v' = 0$ and that C1, C2, F1, P1–P3 and $F(\bar{L}) > g$ are satisfied. Then there exists a quasi-stationary consistent equilibrium $(\alpha,m,\theta) \gg 0$. Furthermore,

(i)   if $g \geqslant \tau F(\bar{L})$, then $(\alpha,m,\theta) \in I$;
(ii)   if $\tau F(\bar{L}) > g > \tau\Pi(1,\alpha^*)$, then there exists at least one equilibrium $(\alpha,m,\theta) \in I$;
(iii) there exists a unique Walrasian equilibrium $(\alpha^*,m^*,1)$ if and only if $g = \tau\Pi(1,\alpha^*)$;
(iv) if $g < \tau\Pi(1,\alpha^*)$, then $(\alpha,m,\theta) \in K$.

The proof is fairly long and requires only standard fixed point arguments. Therefore only the essential steps will be given.

Proof   If (α,m,θ) is a quasi-stationary consistent equilibrium with associated signals (s^ℓ,s^c), one finds immediately that α has an upper bound $\bar{\alpha} < F'[F^{-1}(g)] + \varepsilon$, since $(\alpha,m,\theta) \notin C$. This yields employment levels $F^{-1}(g) \leqslant \mathscr{L}(\alpha,m,\theta,\theta) \leqslant L$. Then P2 essentially implies a lower bound $\underline{s}^\ell$ on the labour market signal with $-1 < \underline{s}^\ell \leqslant s^\ell$ which in turns yields a positive lower bound on θ, i.e. $0 < \underline{\theta} = w(\underline{s}^\ell) \leqslant w[\sigma^\ell(\alpha,m,\theta,\theta)] = p[\sigma^c(\alpha,m,\theta,\theta)] = \theta$. Then, $m \leqslant F(\bar{L})/\underline{\theta}$. The continuity of p implies an upper bound $\bar{\theta}$ for θ. Hence, the continuous mapping $\psi : \mathbb{R}^3_+ \to \mathbb{R}^3_+$ defined by

$$\psi_1 (\alpha,m,\theta) = a(m,\theta)$$

$$\psi_2 (\alpha,m,\theta) = \frac{1}{\theta}\{\min\{m+g, F(L)\} - \tau[F(L) - \alpha L]\}$$

$$\psi_3 (\alpha,m,\theta) = 1 + p[\sigma^c(\alpha,m,\theta,\theta)]$$

such that

$$L = \mathcal{L}(\alpha,m,\theta,\theta)$$

has a fixed point in the interior of an appropriately chosen compact cube $K = [0,k]^3$. Therefore, a quasi-stationary consistent equilibrium $(\alpha,m,\theta) \gg 0$ exists.

(i)   If $g \geqslant \tau F(\bar{L})$, then all Keynesian and the Walrasian equilibrium have a positive deficit. Therefore, $(\alpha,m,\theta) \in I$.

(ii) if $\tau F(\bar{L}) > g > \tau\Pi(1,\alpha^*) = \tau[F(\bar{L}) - \alpha^*\bar{L}]$, there exists $0 < \tilde{\alpha} < \alpha^*$ such that $g = \tau[F(\bar{L}) - \tilde{\alpha}\bar{L}]$. Then replacing the mapping ψ_1 by $\tilde{\psi}_1 = \max\{\tilde{\alpha},\psi_1\}$ yields a fixed point $(\alpha,m,\theta) \in I$ with $\alpha > \tilde{\alpha}$ and $\theta > 1$.

(iii) $g = \tau\Pi(1,\alpha^*)$ implies that $(\alpha^*,m^*,1)$ is Walrasian when
$$m^* = F[h(\alpha^*)] - g - c^w(1,\alpha^*\bar{L}) - c^s[1,(1-\tau)\Pi(1,\alpha^*)].$$

(iv) If $g < \tau\Pi(1,\alpha^*)$, then taxes in all I states are larger than g. Therefore the Walrasian equilibrium as well as all I states have a government surplus, so that only Keynesian equilibria are possible.

QED

The economic implications of theorem 5.4 are fairly strong and they may be somewhat surprising. The features listed under (ii)–(iv) imply that the disequilibrium type of any steady state consistent with the law of supply and demand is essentially determined only by the government parameters (g,τ) and profits under labour market clearing. More precisely, the sign of the government deficit under labour market clearing in temporary equilibrium determines essentially the type of disequilibrium in quasi-stationary states. Therefore, agents' expectations play no role whatsoever.

Statement (ii) of theorem 5.4 does not exclude the possibility that there may exist states of repressed inflation and Keynesian unemployment states at the same time. Both types of equilibria require a real wage less than α^*. For a Keynesian unemployment equilibrium this means that $w[\sigma^l(\alpha,m,\theta,\theta)] = p[\sigma^c(\alpha,m,\theta,\theta)] < 0$ but there is a positive notional excess demand on the labour market, i.e. $h(\alpha) > L$. Such a possibility is not excluded by assumption P3, but it implies that notional excess does not lead to a real wage decrease. If this property is excluded by the adjustment and signalling functions, then type uniqueness of quasi-stationary consistent equilibria follows for all three distinct deficit situations under labour market clearing.

Theorem 5.5

Assume that $v' = 0$ and that C1, C2, F1 and P1 are satisfied. If (α,m,θ) and

$$w[\sigma'(\alpha,m,\theta,\theta)] = p[\sigma^c(\alpha,m,\theta,\theta)] < 0$$

imply $\alpha \geq \alpha^*$, then all quasi-stationary consistent equilibria are of the same disequilibrium type and

(i) $(\alpha,m,\theta) \in K$	if and only if	$g < \tau\Pi(1,\alpha^*)$
(ii) $(\alpha,m,\theta) = WE$	if and only if	$g = \tau\Pi(1,\alpha^*)$
(iii) $(\alpha,m,\theta) \in I$	if and only if	$g > \tau\Pi(1,\alpha^*)$.

Proof It is sufficient to prove that there are no two quasi-stationary consistent equilibria (α_1,m_1,θ_1) and (α_2,m_2,θ_2) of different types for any given (g,τ). Suppose the contrary and let

$$L_1 = \mathcal{L}(\alpha_1,m_1,\theta_1,\theta_1) \leq \mathcal{L}_2(\alpha_2,m_2,\theta_2,\theta_2) = \bar{L},$$

$$\theta_1 < \theta_2 \text{ and } \alpha_1 \geq \alpha^* \geq \alpha_2.$$

Then

$$\tau[F(L_1) - \alpha_1 L_1] \leq \tau\Pi(1,\alpha^*)$$
$$\leq \tau[F(\bar{L}) - \alpha_2\bar{L}].$$

Moreover,

$$0 \geq m_1(\theta_1 - 1) = g - \tau[F(L_1) - \alpha_1 L_1]$$
$$0 \leq m_2(\theta_2 - 1) = g - \tau[F(\bar{L}) - \alpha_2\bar{L}]$$
$$+ \min\{0, F(\bar{L}) - g - m_2\}$$

where one of the inequalities is strict. Then,

$$0 < m_2(\theta_2 - 1) - m_1(\theta_1 - 1)$$
$$\leq - \tau[F(\bar{L}) - \alpha_2\bar{L}] + \tau[F(L_1) - \alpha_1 L_1]$$
$$\leq \tau[-\Pi(1,\alpha^*) + \Pi(1,\alpha^*)] = 0$$

which is a contradiction.

QED

The additional assumption of the theorem is satisfied for a large class of adjustment and signalling functions. For example, for the explicit signalling functions of the preceding section, there exist linear functions w and p and a constant $0 < \underline{\delta} < 1$ such that $p[\sigma^c(\alpha^*,m,\theta,\theta)] \geq w[\sigma^c(\alpha^*,m,\theta,\theta)]$ holds for all $(\alpha^*,m,\theta,\theta) \in K$, if $w = \delta p$ and $\delta \leq \underline{\delta}$. Finally, for the case of a proportional income tax, type uniqueness requires no additional assumption and follows immediately from the fact that tax revenue is monotonic in the employment level.

To conclude this section a more detailed comparison of the results here with the findings of some of the contributions of the literature may be informative. The paper closest to the prototype model is due to Michel and Picard (1982). Except for their choice of a continuous time setting, their model describes an economy with constant labour supply, atemporal production, government demand, and money creation through government deficits. The temporary structure is defined by an employment function which displays a partition of (α,m) -space with essentially the same features as figure 5.2. Their price and wage adjustment mechanism is a proper convex combination of an expectations-augmented version of the law of supply and demand and of monopolistic wage and price setting by workers and capitalists respectively. They establish existence and type uniqueness of quasi-stationary equilibria for all three types of disequilibrium situations, including classical unemployment. It is evident that this last possibility requires that the monopolistic price and wage setting parameters must be sufficiently large to overcompensate the effects from the law of supply and demand. In fact, if the influence of the monopolistic elements is reduced, the quasi-stationary classical unemployment equilibria disappear and their results confirm the features here, i.e. positive inflation occurs only under states of repressed inflation and Keynesian unemployment states are associated with negative inflation.

One of their major results is a negatively sloped long-run Phillips curve which has branches of classical and Keynesian unemployment for positive inflation. For the whole model the rate of inflation is considered as a government control variable while they interpret a simple linear aggregate demand function as one with constant government real demand. The linear form can be criticized as well as the suppression of the budget constraints for consumers and the government. Clearly, taxes must be lump sum and endogenous. But this is not made explicit. It would be interesting to investigate whether the monopolistic price and wage setting along with a consistent microeconomic description of the consumption sector and an explicit modelling of taxes could be identified as the sole cause of a negatively sloped Phillips curve.

A second paper by Fourgeaud and Michel (1982) also discusses the law of supply and demand within a continuous time setting where the model is expanded to include capital accumulation but no population growth. In essence they also show that steady states do not show a long-run trade-off between positive inflation and employment if the law of supply and demand prevails. They observe that Keynesian unemployment steady states are associated with deflation and a permanent government budget surplus. However, they seem to conclude that this implies that ' . . . the tendency to long-run full employment under competitive adjustments is of a general nature' (own translation). This can only be true if a specific government policy prevails. In a second model Fourgeaud and Michel introduce mark-up pricing and complete wage indexation to inflation. For this case they show that quasi-stationary equilibria may fail to exist or they are not of the Keynesian unemployment type.

A third paper by Picard (1983) introduces capital accumulation and population growth combined with an expectation-augmented law of supply and demand for the price adjustment. For the wage adjustment the law is also augmented by a term which sets a target real wage. The major result of the paper is a downward-sloping long-run Phillips curve which associates positive inflation with unemployment either of the classical type or with states on the boundary between Keynesian and classical unemployment. For the case of zero population growth the results seem to imply that long-run Keynesian unemployment can only occur with deflation.

Summarizing the results of the three papers, Michel and Picard present the only case of a model with a long-run Phillips curve associating positive inflation with Keynesian unemployment. Since their monopolistic price and wage adjustment rules are somewhat *ad hoc* and some other features are chosen quite arbitrarily, it remains an open and challenging question whether the long-run inflation–unemployment trade-off can be derived under a more consistent framework.

5.6 Beyond the Prototype

The introduction to chapter 4 listed some important issues which, in order to be treated, required extensions of the prototype model. These were in particular capital accumulation, inventory holdings, bonds or public debt, transactions constraints and private credit. All these imply considerable changes of the prototype model. The description of the dynamic features of any of these extended models requires the solution of a large number of open problems. If one applies the same criterion of a rigorous and consistent microeconomic formulation as in the prototype model a search in the literature for contributions is in vain. The few existing publications contain some partial results.

The volume edited by Hénin and Michel (1982) contains several contributions which describe neoclassical continuous time growth models in disequilibrium. The paper by Picard (1983) is very similar to his contribution in (1982). It is evident that the formulation of the investment behaviour of firms is a crucial element in all these models. The differences in the results should be attributed to a large extent to the discretionary choices. On a more fundamental conceptual level one may question the choice of continuous time as the appropriate dynamic framework when the underlying economic entities and concepts are essentially of a discrete nature. It is well known that a consistent continuous-time model equivalent to one of discrete time requires additional flow and stock constraints for all time (see, for example, Turnovsky , 1977). To demonstrate such equivalence may entail a delicate conceptual task and considerable mathematical effort. Again the challenge remains to incorporate capital accumulation into the prototype model and to compare its features with the results provided in the whole volume.

Essentially only two papers have considered the dynamics of inventory holding in the framework of a temporary equilibrium model with quantity rationing. Honkapohja and Ito (1981) construct a linearized model of demand and inventory adjustment which lacks a microeconomic foundation. Their analysis is further restricted by the fact that budget constraints and therefore the endogenous wealth dynamics are ignored. Their major result establishes that under fixed prices and wages the existence of a Keynesian unemployment steady state implies cyclical behaviour around it. However, repressed inflation steady states are globally unstable. Steady states in the classical and in the underconsumption region do not exist. Such an asymmetry between the long-run behaviour of the Keynesian and the repressed inflation regions was also found by Böhm (1978, 1981b) and Honkapohja (1979) for the money adjustment process in models without inventories. However, it is questionable whether this feature is a typical property of any stock adjustment model where money balances and/or inventories are analysed. It is unclear whether the results of the prototype model presented in sections 5.3 and 5.4 confirm these properties.

The second paper by Böhm (1981b) attempts a description of the long-run behaviour of inventories and money balances in a consistently formulated model with one producer, one consumer and no government. Thus, aggregate money balances are constant, but their distribution changes along the disequilibrium path. The paper does not treat price and wage adjustments, but rather assumes that they are fixed at the levels which correspond to a stationary Walrasian equilibrium. Thus, the dynamic analysis is an attempt to isolate the effects of the money balances and inventory adjustment mechanisms from the price and wage adjustment. The overall result of the paper is that, for the particular functional specifications, the joint stock adjustment process is stable and converging to the unique Walrasian equilibrium. There, neither cyclicity nor any form of asymmetry are found. Thus, individual optimizing behaviour in a symmetric setting for consumers and producers does not generate asymmetries of long-run steady states in this particular example. Since there is no government demand nor taxation it is unclear whether deficits and surpluses would change this result. Moreover, the influence of agents' expectations is not analysed. It remains an open question whether the qualitative properties of the prototype model, i.e. in particular the generic multiplicity of quasi-stationary states under perfect foresight, changes or remains in the extended model with inventory holdings.

For a long time the macroeconomic literature concentrated almost exclusively on the short-run effects of fiscal and monetary policy. Until the contributions by Ott and Ott (1965), Christ (1967, 1968), Turnovsky (1977), Blinder and Solow (1973, 1974) and Tobin and Buiter (1976) the long-run effects of the government budget constraint and of wealth composition were largely ignored. As indicated already in the previous sections, there are decisive long-run effects of a money-financed fiscal policy which has an immediate consequence through the government budget constraint. If bonds (i.e. government debt) are incorporated in the model as well, a change of government control variables implies additional effects from a non-balanced government budget, which in turn induce changes in the stock of financial assets until the economy settles down at a new steady state. The importance of these effects was demonstrated most forcefully by Blinder and Solow as well as by Tobin and Buiter within the standard IS–LM framework. Their functional forms and their behavioural equations, however, are given very much in an *ad hoc* way. Moreover, these authors discuss all issues within a complete fixed price model where neither commodity prices nor wages adjust. With respect to both issues, the prototype model with the extension of chapter 4 offers an improvement. The demand functions for assets are derived from utility maximizing agents. In addition, price and wage adjustments according to the law of supply and demand can be incorporated in the same way as in section 5.4. The steady state analysis under perfect foresight is dealt with explicitly below.

The introduction of interest-bearing government bonds into the prototype model in chapter 4 made the model closest to the standard Keynesian framework. It was shown there that, under the standard assumption with the bond market always clearing, the short-run employment multipliers of fiscal and monetary policies had the same signs as in the standard IS–LM framework with a reversed effect on the interest rate. It was indicated there, however, that the short-run analysis ignores the subsequent wealth effects of a once and for all change in government debt. This issue will be taken up here again. It will be shown that in many cases the short-run effect of an expansionary monetary policy implies a contractionary long-run effect if steady states for the same once and for all change in government real debt are considered. This result will be derived for two cases of Keynesian unemployment with fixed (θ,α) and $\theta \geqslant 1$.

Applying the techniques of chapter 3 this implies that for any period t employment L_t and the bond price q_t are determined by two functions

$$L_t = \mathscr{L}(p_t, w_t, p_{t+1}, M_t, B_t, B_{t+1}, g, \tau, d)$$
$$q_t = q(p_t, w_t, p_{t+1}, M_t, B_t, B_{t+1}, g, \tau, d)$$

where M_t and B_t are the initial private holdings of money and bonds and B_{t+1} is the final bond holding decided upon by the government. Because of the homogeneity properties of the individual demand functions and under perfect foresight on prices these functions can be written as

(i) $L_t = \mathscr{L}(a_t, m_t, \theta_t, b_t, \theta_t b_{t+1})$

(ii) $q_t = q(a_t, m_t, \theta_t, b_t, \theta_t b_{t+1})$ (5.25)

where $b_t = B_t/p_t$ and $b_{t+1} = B_{t+1}/p_{t+1}$, b_t and b_{t+1} denoting real public debt. The variables (g, τ, d) have been eliminated as arguments from the two functions since they are assumed to be constant for the rest of the analysis. Equations (5.23) imply as endogenous money dynamics (assuming no old consumer rationing)

$$m_{t+1}\theta_t = m_t + g + db_t - \tau[F(L_t) - a_t L_t] - q_t(b_{t+1}\theta_t - b_t).$$
(5.26)

Hence, a quasi-stationary state with constant real consumption by young and old consumers and a constant level of employment implies that

(i) $(\theta - 1)(m + qb) = g + db - \tau[F(L) - \alpha L]$

(ii) $L = \mathscr{L}(a, m, \theta, b, \theta b)$ (5.27)

(iii) $q = q(a, m, \theta, b, \theta b)$.

Thus, at a quasi-stationary equilibrium the money stock, nominal public debt, prices and wages all grow at the same rate $\theta - 1$, with the nominal bond price q being constant in all periods. Condition (i) shows quite clearly that with government bonds a stationary equilibrium ($\theta = 1$) requires that taxes have to cover government purchases plus the permanently accruing interest payment db. As before, positive inflation occurs if and only if the government runs a permanent deficit. Moreover, constant nominal government debt is possible if and only if the budget is balanced and $\theta = 1$.

Case 1   Let (a, m, θ, b, q) denote a stationary Keynesian unemployment situation, i.e. $\theta = 1$. Then (5.27)(i) implies that

$$\tau[F(L) - \alpha L] = g + db.$$

Hence, it follows immediately from the stationarity condition that higher nominal public debt in the long run implies higher employment. This result is a sole consequence of the government budget constraint and is therefore independent of any assumption on consumer characteristics. It clearly holds for other tax functions than the profits tax used here, as long as tax revenue is monotonically increasing with employment. More generally, the condition of a balanced budget implies that higher government demand and/or a higher volume of government bonds both imply a higher long-run stationary level of employment. This points to a fundamental difference of the long-run effects of government demand policy and monetary policy through open-market operations. Whereas government demand policy generates a positive employment multiplier both in the short run and in the long run, the effects of an open-market operation are of opposite sign for the short and for the long run. Thus, neglecting the dynamic adjustment through changes in the money stock, and comparing only the two stationary states, any short-run effect on employment of an open-market operation will be reversed intermittently. If the adjustment process is stable, this leads to an opposite long-run effect on employment. The reason for this effect is intuitively clear but generally neglected in traditional Keynesian analysis, since it ignores the government budget constraint. In the short run a change in the volume of government debt creates a direct monetary effect on the bond market and an ensuing effect on employment via the interest rate. However, the interest service of additional government bonds in all subsequent periods has the opposite monetary effect which completely eliminates the short-run effect. Hence, in stationary states with unemployment higher real demand by the government and a higher volume of bonds are both associated with a higher level of employment. These findings confirm the results by Blinder and Solow and by Tobin and Buiter and the long-run policy multipliers here are equivalent to theirs.

Under some additional assumptions these results extend to quasi-stationary states, i.e. to situations with constant rates of inflation and a permanently growing stock of money and nominal debt.

Case 2   Let (α,m,θ,b,q), $\theta > 1$, denote a quasi-stationary Keynesian unemployment equilibrium with employment level L and private consumption of young consumers equal to x. Feasibility of the commodity market implies

$$F(L) - g = x + m + b(q + d)$$

where $x = c_u^w(q,\alpha L) + c^s\{q,(1 - \tau)[F(L) - \alpha L]\}$, $b = b_u^w(q,\alpha L) + b^s\{q,(1 - \tau)[F(L) - \alpha L]\}$, and from the budget equation of young consumers $m = \{F(L) - \tau[F(L) - \alpha L] - x\}/\theta - qb$. Separating the two market clearing conditions for the bond market and the commodity market into two equations (as in section 4.2) one obtains

(i) $F(L) - g = c_u(q,L,b)$
(ii) $\qquad b = b_u(q,L)$. $\hspace{4cm}$ (5.28)

c_u is the steady state effective consumption demand including all income and wealth effects and b_u is the effective bond demand function which, because of the overlapping generations structure, has no wealth effects. Condition (i) describes the steady state IS curve whereas (ii) is the steady state analogue to the LM curve. It should be noted that the IS curve no longer involves any wealth variables. This implies that monetary policy does not change the long-run relationship between employment and the bond price which clears the commodity market under effective demand and supply. The following theorem extends the previous result of the long-run effectiveness of monetary policy.

Theorem 5.6

Let C1, C2 and F1 be satisfied and assume that $\theta - 1 = d/q$ holds at the quasi-stationary state. Then a (small) increase in government real debt b raises the steady state employment level L for given (θ,α).

The condition $\theta - 1 = d/q$ is just the equality of the inflation rate and the nominal interest rate on bonds, i.e. a real interest rate on bonds equal to zero. The proof is straightforward and it will be sketched with the help of figure 5.10 which indicates the contrast to figure 4.6 which characterizes the short-run situation. Bond market clearing (5.28)(ii) implies that the bond market clearing locus is an increasing function $q = \tilde{b}(L,b)$ in L which shifts to the right for $b_2 > b_1$. Conversely, commodity market clearing (5.28)(i) defines a function $q = \tilde{c}(L,b)$ which is decreasing in L if the real rate of interest on bonds is equal to zero. Hence, a small increase in government real debt from b_1 to b_2 raises employment from L_1 to L_2 and lowers the bond price from q_1 to q_2. This increases the nominal interest rate d/q and thus increases the real rate to a positive level. Since the two functions $c_u(q,L)$ are differentiable the result holds in a neighbourhood of the condi-

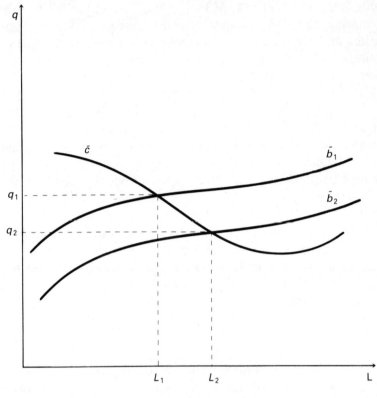

Figure 5.10

tion that the real rate of interest on bonds is equal to zero. However, the partial derivatives of c_u cannot be signed in general for arbitrary real rates of interest. Thus, multiplicity of equilibria and reversal of the effects may occur in general for given (θ, α).

The results of this section confirm that monetary policy in a world of perfect foresight may have long-run employment effects in the same way as fiscal policy. The major source of a positive employment effect is the permanent demand increase generated by higher real interest income. This result was derived for the case of a fixed steady state inflation rate and real wage. However, as the discussion above indicates, the introduction of government bonds increases the possibilities for multiple steady states for the same (θ, α) and for the same policy control variables (g, τ, b) by the government. The same observation was made by Hahn (1980b). This implies again that chances for global monotonic convergence are slim and that one may observe cyclical behaviour.

References and Bibliography

d'Aspremont, C., Dos Santos Ferreira, R. and Gérard-Varet, L. A. 1984: 'Oligopoly and involuntary unemployment'. CORE Discussion Paper No. 8408, Université Catholique de Louvain.

d'Autume, A. 1982: 'Un modèle de croissance en déséquilibre'. In P.-Y. Hénin et P. Michel (eds), *Croissance et Accumulation en Déséquilibre*, Paris: Economica, 213–48.

Azariadis, C. and Böhm, V. 1982: Quantity-constrained equilibria under perfect foresight: some preliminary notes. Mimeograph, Philadelphia.

Balasko, Y. 1979: 'Budget-constraint Pareto-efficient allocations'. *Journal of Economic Theory*, 21, 359–79.

Balasko, Y. 1982: 'Equilibria and efficiency in the fixprice setting'. *Journal of Economic Theory*, 28, 113–27.

Barro, R. J. and Grossman, H. I. 1971: 'A general disequilibrium model of income and employment'. *American Economic Review*, 61, 82–93.

Barro, R. J. and Grossman, H. I. 1974: 'Suppressed inflation and the supply multiplier'. *Review of Economic Studies*, 41, 87–104.

Barro, R. J. and Grossman, H. I. 1976: *Money, Employment and Inflation*. Cambridge: Cambridge University Press.

Benassy, J.-P. 1973: 'Disequilibrium theory'. CRMS Working Paper No. 185, University of California, Berkeley.

Benassy, J.-P. 1975a: 'Disequilibrium exchange in barter and monetary economies'. *Economic Inquiry*, 13, 131–56.

Benassy, J.-P. 1975b: 'Neo-Keynesian disequilibrium theory in a monetary economy'. *Review of Economic Studies*, 42, 503–24.

Benassy, J.-P. 1976a: 'The disequilibrium approach to monopolistic price setting and general monopolistic equilibrium'. *Review of Economic Studies*, 43, 69–81.

Benassy, J.-P. 1976b: 'Théorie du déséquilibre et fondements microéconomiques de la macroéconomie'. *Revue Économique*, 27, 755–804.

Benassy, J.-P. 1977a: 'A neo-Keynesian model of price and quantity determination in disequilibrium'. In G. Schwödiauer (ed.), *Equilibrium and Disequilibrium in Economic Theory*, Dordrecht: Reidel, 511–44.

Benassy, J.-P. 1977b: 'On quantity signals and the foundations of effective demand theory'. *Scandinavian Journal of Economics*, 79, 147–68.

Benassy, J.-P. 1982a: 'Developments in non-Walrasian economics and the microeconomic foundations of macroeconomics'. In W. Hildenbrand (ed.), *Advances in Economic Theory*, Cambridge: Cambridge University Press, 121–46.

Benassy, J.-P. 1982b: *The Economics of Market Disequilibrium*. San Diego, CA: Academic Press.

Benassy, J.-P. 1983: 'The three regimes of the IS–LM model'. *European Economic Review*, 23, 1–17.

Benassy, J.-P. 1984a: *Macroéconomie et Théorie du Déséquilibre*. Paris: Dunod.

Benassy, J.-P. 1984b: 'A non-Walrasian model of the business cycle'. *Journal of Economic Behavior and Organization*, 5, 77–89.

Benassy, J.-P. 1986: *Macroeconomics: An Introduction to the Non-Walrasian Approach*. San Diego, CA: Academic Press.

Bergstrom, T. C. 1986: 'The core when strategies are restricted by law'. *Review of Economic Studies*, 42 (2), No. 130, 249–58.

Blad, M. and Zeeman, Ch. 1982: 'Oscillations between repressed inflation and Keynesian equilibria due to inertia in decision making'. *Journal of Economic Theory*, 28, 165–82.

Blanchard, O. J. 1984: 'Current and anticipated deficits, interest rates and economic activity'. *European Economic Review*, 25, 7–27.

Blinder, A. S. 1981: 'Inventories and the structure of macro models'. *Papers and Proceedings*, 71, American Economic Association, 11–17.

Blinder, A. S. 1982: 'Inventories and sticky prices: more on the microfoundations of macroeconomics'. *American Economic Review*, 72, 334–48.

Blinder, A. S. and Solow, R. M. 1973: 'Does fiscal policy matter'. *Journal of Public Economics*, 2, 319–37.

Blinder, A. S. and Solow, R. M. 1974: 'Analytical foundations of fiscal policy'. In *The Economics of Public Finance*, Washington, DC: Brookings Institution, 3–115.

Böhm, V. 1978: 'Disequilibrium dynamics in a simple macroeconomic model'. *Journal of Economic Theory*, 17, 179–99.

Böhm, V. 1979: A simple macroeconomic disequilibrium model. Mimeograph, Mannheim.

Böhm, V. 1980: *Preise, Löhne und Beschäftigung. Beiträge zur Theorie der mikroökonomischen Grundlagen der Makroökonomik*. Tübingen: J. C. B. Mohr (Paul Siebeck).

Böhm, V. 1981a: Prices and wages in a simple macroeconomic disequilibrium model. Mimeograph, Mannheim.

Böhm, V. 1981b: 'Inventories and money balances in a dynamic model with rationing'. CARESS Working Paper No. 81–15, University of Pennsylvania.

Böhm, V. 1982: 'On the uniqueness of macroeconomic equilibria with quantity rationing'. *Economics Letters*, 10, 43–8.

Böhm, V. 1983: 'Quantity rationing vs. IS–LM – a synthesis'. Discussion Paper No. 252/83, Institut für Volkswirtschaftslehre und Statistik, Universität Mannheim.

Böhm, V. 1984: 'Fixed prices, rationing and optimality'. CARESS Working Paper No. 84–10, University of Pennsylvania.

Böhm, V. 1987: 'Inflation, Beschäftigung und Staatsnachfrage'. In R. Henn (ed.), *Technologie, Wachstum und Beschäftigung*, Berlin: Springer, 984–9.

Böhm, V. and Keiding, H. 1986: 'Inflation and welfare in international trade'. CORE Discussion Paper No. 8601, Université Catholique de Louvain.

Böhm, V. and Lévine, P. 1979: 'Temporary equilibria with quantity rationing'. *Review of Economic Studies*, 46, 361–77.

Böhm, V. and Müller, H. 1977: 'Two examples of equilibria under price rigidities and quantity rationing'. *Zeitschrift für Nationalökonomie*, 37, 165–73.

Böhm, V. and Puhakka, M. 1988: 'Rationing and optimality in overlapping generations models'. *Scandinavian Journal of Economics*, 90, 225–32.

Böhm, V. and Maskin, E., Polemarchakis, H. and Postlewaite, A. 1983: 'Monopolistic quantity rationing'. *Quarterly Journal of Economics*, 98 (supplement), 189–98.

Christ, C. F. 1967: 'A short-run aggregate-demand model of the interdependence and effects of monetary and fiscal policies with Keynesian and classical interest elasticities'. *American Economic Review*, 57, 434–43.

Christ, C. F. 1968: 'A simple macroeconomic model with a government budget restraint'. *Journal of Political Economy*, 76, 53–67.

Clower, R. W. 1965: 'The Keynesian counter-revolution: a theoretical appraisal'. In F. M. Hahn and F. P. R. Brechling (eds), *The Theory of Interest Rates*, London: Macmillan, 103–25.

Clower, R. W. 1967: 'A reconsideration of the microfoundations of monetary theory'. *Western Economic Journal*, 6, 1–8.

Danthine, J.-P. and Peytrignet, M. 1981: 'Intégration de l'analyse graphique IS–LM avec la théorie des équilibres à prix fixes: une note pédagogique'. In G. Bramoullé et J.-P. Giran (eds), *Analyse du Déséquilibre*, Paris: Economica, 115–35.

Danthine, J.-P. and Peytrignet, M. 1984: 'Complement to: rationing macroeconomics: a graphical exposition: aggregate demand and supply'. *European Economic Review*, 26, 203–8.

Dehez, P. 1982: 'Stationary Keynesian equilibria'. *European Economic Review*, 19, 245–58.

Dehez, P. 1985: 'Monopolistic equilibrium and involuntary unemployment'. *Journal of Economic Theory*, 36, 160–5.

Dehez, P. and Drèze, J. H. 1984: 'On supply constrained equilibria'. *Journal of Economic Theory*, 33, 172–82.

Dehez, P. and Gabszewicz, J. J. 1977: 'On the convergence of sequences of disequilibria'. CORE Discussion Paper No. 7701, Université Catholique de Louvain.

Dehez, P. and Gabszewicz, J. J. 1979: 'On disequilibrium savings and public consumption'. *Zeitschrift für Nationalökonomie*, 39, 53–61.

Dixit, A. 1976: 'Public finance in a Keynesian temporary equilibrium'. *Journal of Economic Theory*, 12, 242–58.

Dixit, A. 1978: 'The balance of trade in a model of temporary equilibrium with rationing'. *Review of Economic Studies*, 45, 393–404.

Drazen, A. 1980: 'Recent developments in macroeconomic disequilibrium theory'. *Econometrica*, 48, 283–306.

Drèze, J. H. 1974: *Allocation under Uncertainty: Equilibrium and Optimality*. London: Macmillan.

Drèze, J. H. 1975: 'Existence of an exchange equilibrium under price rigidities'. *International Economic Review*, 16, 301–20.

Drèze, J. H. and Müller, H. 1980: 'Optimality properties of rationing schemes'. *Journal of Economic Theory*, 23, 131–49.

Eckalbar, J. C. 1979: 'Stability with medium of exchange constraints and spillovers'. *Oxford Economic Papers*, 31, 386–402.

Eckalbar, J. C. 1980: 'The stability of non-Walrasian processes: two examples'. *Econometrica*, 48, 371–86.

Eichberger, J. 1983a: 'Temporary equilibria with firms and government'. Discussion Paper No. 268/83, Institut für Volkswirtschaftslehre und Statistik, Universität Mannheim.

Eichberger, J. 1983b: Does the fiscal stimulus depress employment? On a neglected effect in traditional macroeconomics. Mimeograph, Mannheim.

Eichberger, J. 1984a: *Geld und Kredit in einer Ökonomie mit festen Preisen. Ein ökonomischer Beitrag zur keynesianischen Unterbeschäftigungstheorie*. Frankfurt: Lang.

Eichberger, J. 1984b: 'Temporary equilibrium with bankruptcy'. Research Report No. 8419, University of Western Ontario, London, Canada.

Eichberger, J. 1985: Government policy and unemployment. Mimeograph, Canberra.

Eichberger, J. 1986: 'On the efficacy of fiscal policy'. *Annales d'Economie et de Statistique*, 3, 151–68.

Felderer, B. and Homburg, St. 1984: *Makroökonomik und neue Makroökonomik*. Berlin: Springer.

Fourgeaud, C. and Michel, P. 1982: 'Une analyse dynamique de déséquilibre'. In P.-Y. Hénin et P. Michel (eds), *Croissance et Accumulation en Déséquilibre*, Paris: Economica, 109–46.

Fourgeaud, C., Lenclud, B. and Michel, P. 1979: 'Two-Sector model with quantity rationing'. CEPREMAP, Discussion Paper No. 7913, Paris.

Futia, C. 1977: 'Excess supply equilibria'. *Journal of Economic Theory*, 14, 200–20.

Gale, D. 1978: 'A note on conjectural equilibria'. *Review of Economic Studies*, 45, 33–8.

Gale, D. 1979: 'Large economies with trading uncertainty'. *Review of Economic Studies*, 46, 319–38.

Gale, D. 1983: *Money: In Disequilibrium*. Cambridge: Cambridge University Press.

Glustoff, E. 1968: 'On the existence of a Keynesian equilibrium'. *Review of Economic Studies*, 35, 327–34.

Grandmont, J.-M. 1974: 'On the short-run equilibrium in a monetary economy'. In J. H. Drèze (ed.), *Allocation under Uncertainty: Equilibrium and Optimality*, London: Macmillan, 213–28.

Grandmont, J.-M. 1977a: 'Temporary general equilibrium theory'. *Econometrica*, 45, 535–72.

Grandmont, J.-M. 1977b: 'The logic of the fixed-price method'. *Scandinavian Journal of Economics*, 79, 168–86.

Grandmont, J.-M. 1982a: 'Temporary general equilibrium theory'. In K. J. Arrow and M. D. Intriligator (eds), *Handbook of Mathematical Economics*, Amsterdam: North Holland, 879–922.

Grandmont, J.-M. 1982b: 'Classical and Keynesian unemployment in the IS–LM model'. CEPREMAP, Discussion Paper No. 8216, Paris.

Grandmont, J.-M. 1983: *Money and Value. A Reconsideration of Classical and Neoclassical Monetary Theories*. Cambridge: Cambridge University Press.

Grandmont, J.-M. and Laroque, G. 1975: 'On money and banking'. *Review of Economic Studies*, 42, 207–36.

Grandmont, J.-M. and Laroque, G. 1976a: 'On temporary Keynesian equilibria'. *Review of Economic Studies*, 43, 53–67.

Grandmont, J.-M. and Laroque, G. 1976b: 'On the liquidity trap'. *Econometrica*, 44, 129–35.

Grandmont, J.-M. and Laroque, G. 1977: 'On temporary Keynesian equilibrium'. In G.-C. Harcourt (ed.), *The Microeconomic Foundations of Macroeconomics*, Boulder, CO: Westview Press, 41–61.

Green, J. 1974: 'Preexisting contracts and temporary general equilibrium'. In M. Balch, D. McFadden and S. Wu (eds), *Essays on Economic Behavior under Uncertainty, Contributions to Economic Analysis*, Amsterdam: North Holland, 263–86.

Green, J. 1980: 'On the theory of effective demand'. *Economic Journal*, 90, 341–53.

Green, J. and Polemarchakis, H. 1976: 'A brief note on the efficiency of equilibria with costly transactions'. *Review of Economic Studies*, 43, 537–42.

Grossman, H. I. 1977: 'Money, interest, and prices in market disequilibrium'. *Journal of Political Economy*, 79, 943–61.

Gurley, J. G. and Shaw, E. S. 1971: *Money in a Theory of Finance.* Washington, DC: Brookings Institution.

Haga, H. 1976: *A Disequilibrium Model with Money and Bonds: A Keynesian–Walrasian Synthesis.* Berlin: Springer.

Hahn, F. 1982: *Money and Inflation.* Oxford: Basil Blackwell.

Hahn, F. H. 1977: 'Exercises in conjectural equilibria'. *Scandinavian Journal of Economics*, 79, 210–26.

Hahn, F. H. 1978: 'On non-Walrasian equilibria'. *Review of Economic Studies*, 45, 1–17.

Hahn, F. H. 1980a: 'Unemployment from a theoretic viewpoint'. *Economica*, 47, 285–98.

Hahn, F. H. 1980b: 'Monetarism and economic theory'. *Economica*, 47, 1–17.

Hahn, F. H. and Brechling, F. P. R. 1965: *The Theory of Interest Rates*, Proceedings of a conference held by the International Economic Association. London: Macmillan.

Hart, O. 1982: 'A model of imperfect competition with Keynesian features'. *Quarterly Journal of Economics*, 97, 109–38.

Hart, O. D. 1983: 'Economic fluctuations with an imperfectly competitive labour market'. In J.-P. Fitoussi (ed.), *Modern Macroeconomic Theory*, Oxford: Basil Blackwell, 153–70.

Heller, W. P. and Starr, R. M. 1979: 'Unemployment equilibrium with myopic complete information'. *Review of Economic Studies*, 46, 339–59.

Hénin, P.-Y. and Michel, P. 1982: *Croissance et Accumulation en Déséquilibre.* Paris: Economica.

Hénin, P.-Y. and Michel, P. 1984: 'The four regimes of a disequilibrium IS–LM model: a three dimensional analysis'. Document No. 83, Centre de Recherche Conjoncture et Analyse des Déséquilibres, Paris.

Hicks, J. 1946: *Value and Capital.* Oxford: Clarendon Press.

Hicks, J. 1965: *Capital and Growth.* Oxford: Oxford University Press.

Hildenbrand, K. and Hildenbrand, W. 1978: 'On Keynesian equilibria with unemployment'. *Journal of Economic Theory*, 18, 255–77.

Honkapohja, S. 1979: 'On the dynamics of disequilibrium in a macromodel with flexible wages and prices'. In M. Aoki and A. Marzollo (eds), *New Trends in Dynamic System Theory and Economics*, San Diego, CA: Academic Press, 303–36.

Honkapohja, S. 1980a: 'The employment multiplier after disequilibrium dynamics'. *Scandinavian Journal of Economics*, 81, 1–14.

Honkapohja, S. 1980b: 'A note on monopolistic quantity rationing'. *Economics Letters*, 6, 203–9.

Honkapohja, S. and Ito, T. 1981: 'Inventory dynamics in a simple disequilibrium macroeconomic model'. *Scandinavian Journal of Economics*, 82, 184–98.

Honkapohja, S. and Ito, T. 1983: 'Stability with regime switching'. *Journal of Economic Theory*, 29, 22–48.

Honkapohja, S. and Ito, T. 1985: 'On macroeconomic equilibrium with stochastic rationing'. *Scandinavian Journal of Economics*, 87, 66–88.

Hool, B. 1976: 'Money, expectations and the existence of a temporary equilibrium'. *Review of Economic Studies*, 43, 439–45.

Hool, B. 1979: 'Liquidity, speculation, and the demand for money'. *Journal of Economic Theory*, 21, 73–87.

Hool, B. 1980: 'Monetary and fiscal policies in short run equilibria with rationing'. *International Economic Review*, 21, 301–16.

Howard, D. H. 1977: 'Rationing, quantity constraints, and consumption theory'. *Econometrica*, 45, 399–412.

Ito, T. 1980: 'Disequilibrium growth theory'. *Journal of Economic Theory*, 23, 380–409.

Iwai, K. 1974: 'The firm in uncertain markets and its price, wage and employment adjustments'. *Review of Economic Studies*, 41, 257–76.

John, R. 1985: 'A remark on conjectural equilibria'. *Scandinavian Journal of Economics*, 87, 137–41.

Kades, E. A. 1985: 'Dynamics of fixprice models'. Working Paper 8505, Federal Reserve Bank of Cleveland.

Korliras, P. G. 1975: 'A disequilibrium macroeconomic model'. *Quarterly Journal of Economics*, 89, 56–80.

Kosch, B. 1981: 'On the global uniqueness of fix-price equilibria'. Discussion Paper No. 184-81, Institut für Volkswirtschaftslehre und Statistik, Universität Mannheim.

Kurz, M. 1982: 'Unemployment equilibrium in an economy with linked prices'. *Journal of Economic Theory*, 26, 100–23.

Laroque, G. 1986: 'On the inventory cycle and the instability of the competitive mechanism'. Financial Research Center Memorandum No. 67, Princeton University.

Laussel, D. 1982: 'Sentiers de croissance en déséquilibre'. In P.-Y. Hénin et P. Michel (eds), *Croissance et Accumulation en Déséquilibre*, Paris: Economica, 183–212.

Leijonhufvud, A. 1968: *On Keynesian Economics and the Economics of Keynes. A Study in Monetary Theory*. London: Oxford University Press.

Lucas, R. E. Jr. 1980: 'Equilibrium in a pure currency economy'. *Economic Inquiry*, 18, 203–20.

Malinvaud, E. 1977: *The Theory of Unemployment Reconsidered*. Oxford: Basil Blackwell.

Malinvaud, E. 1980: *Profitability and Unemployment*. Cambridge: Cambridge University Press.

Malinvaud, E. 1981: *Théorie Macroéconomique*, vol. 1, *Comportements, Croissance*. Paris: Dunod.

Malinvaud, E. 1982: *Théorie Macroéconomique*, vol. 2, *Evolutions Conjoncturelles*. Paris: Dunod.

Malinvaud, E. and Younès, Y. 1977: 'Some new concepts for the microeconomic foundations of macroeconomics'. In G. C. Harcourt (ed.), *The Microeconomic Foundations of Macroeconomics*, Boulder, CO: Westview Press. 62–85.

Michel, P. 1982: 'Expected equilibrium and fix-price equilibrium in a simple macroeconomic model: equivalence theorems and stability'. *Recherches Economiques de Louvain*, 48 (1), 57–76.

Michel, P. and Picard, P. 1982: 'Ajustements inflationnistes et déséquilibres'. In P.-Y. Hénin et P. Michel (eds), *Croissance et Accumulation en Déséquilibre*, Paris: Economica, 17–44.

Michel, P. and Schioppa, F. P. 1983: 'A dynamic macroeconomic model with monopolistic behavior in the labor market'. *European Economic Review*, 22, 331–50.

Modigliani, F. 1961: 'Long-run implications of alternative fiscal policies and the burden of the national debt'. *Economic Journal*, 71, 730–55.

Modigliani, F. 1963: 'The monetary mechanism and its interaction with real phenomena'. *Review of Economics and Statistics*, 45, S79–107.

Muellbauer, J. and Portes, R. 1978: 'Macroeconomic models with quantity rationing'. *Economic Journal*, 88, 788–821.

Müller, H. H. 1983: *Fiscal Policies in a General Equilibrium Model with Persistent Unemployment*. Berlin: Springer.

Neary, J. P. and Roberts, K. W. S. 1980: 'The theory of household behaviour under rationing'. *European Economic Review*, 13, 25–42.

Neary, J. P. and Stiglitz, J. E. 1983: 'Toward a reconstruction of Keynesian economics: expectations and constrained equilibria'. *Quarterly Journal of Economics*, 98, 199–228.

Negishi, T. 1960: 'Monopolistic competition and general equilibrium'. *Review of Economic Studies*, 28, 196–201.

Negishi, T. 1978: 'Existence of an under-employment equilibrium'. In G. Schwödiauer (ed.), *Equilibrium and Disequilibrium in Economic Theory*, Dordrecht: Reidel, 497–510.

Negishi, T. 1979: *Microeconomic Foundations of Keynesian Macroeconomics*. Amsterdam: North Holland.

Ott, D. J. and Ott, A. 1965: 'Budget balance and equilibrium income'. *Journal of Finance*, 20, 71–7.

Patinkin, D. 1965: *Money, Interest and Prices: An Integration of Monet-*

ary and Value Theory, second edition. New York: Harper & Row.

Peeters, M. 1983: 'Keynesian phenomena in a sequence economy: unsatisfactory equilibria and the real balance effect'. Institute for Economic Research Discussion Paper Series No. 8312/G, Erasmus University, Rotterdam.

Peytrignet, M. 1985: 'Is classical unemployment a rule?' CORE Discussion Paper No. 8535, Université Catholique de Louvain.

Phlips, L. 1983: *Des Fondements Microéconomiques de la Macroéconomie*. Cahiers du Départment d'Économétrie No. 83.01, Université de Genève.

Picard, P. 1982: 'Inflation, croissance et déséquilibre'. In P.-Y. Hénin and P. Michel (eds), *Croissance et Accumulation en Déséquilibre*, Paris: Economica, 147–82.

Picard, P. 1983: 'Inflation and growth in a disequilibrium macroeconomic model'. *Journal of Economic Theory*, 30, 266–95.

Ramser, H. J. 1978: 'Rationale Erwartungen und Wirtschaftspolitik'. *Zeitschrift für die Gesamte Staatswissenschaft*, 134, 57–72.

Ramser, H. J. 1984: 'Konjunkturtheorie auf der Grundlage temporären Gleichgewichts bei Mengenrationierung'. In G. Bombach, B. Gahlen and A. E. Ott (eds), *Perspektiven der Konjunkturforschung*, Schriftenreihe des Wirtschaftswissenschaftlichen Seminars Ottobeuren, vol. 13, Tübingen: Mohr, 63–84.

Ramser, H. J. 1986: 'Keynes-Literatur und die Relevanz makroökonomischer Lehrbuchmodelle'. *Jahrbücher für Nationalökonomie und Statistik*, 201/5, 441–56.

Rankin, N. 1985: 'Taxation versus spending as the fiscal instrument for demand management: a disequilibrium welfare approach'. Discussion Paper No. 145, Department of Economics, Queen Mary College, University of London.

Riese, H. 1985: 'Keynes' Geldtheorie'. In H. Scherf (ed.), *Studien zur Entwicklung der ökonomischen Theorie*, vol. 4, Berlin: Duncker und Humblot, 9–26.

Roberts, K. 1982: 'Desirable Fiscal Policies under Keynesian Unemployment'. *Oxford Economic Papers*, 34, 1–22.

Rothschild, K. W. 1981: *Einführung in die Ungleichgewichtstheorie*. Berlin: Springer.

Sargent, T. J. 1979: *Macroeconomic Theory*. San Diego, CA: Academic Press.

Schmachtenberg, R. 1987: 'Monopolistic equilibria and voluntary trading'. Discussion Paper No. 346–87, Universität Mannheim.

Schulz, N. 1982: 'Existence of equilibria without Walras' law and homogeneity'. Working Paper 8211, Universität Dortmund.

Schulz, N. 1985: 'Existence of equilibria based on continuity and boundary behaviour'. *Economics Letters*, 19, 101–3.

Silvestre, J. 1982a: 'Ambiguities in the sign of excess effective demand by firms'. *Review of Economic Studies*, 49, 645–51.

Silvestre, J. 1982b: 'Fixprice analysis in exchange economies'. *Journal of Economic Theory*, 26, 28–58.

Silvestre, J. 1983: 'Fixprice analysis in productive economies'. *Journal of Economic Theory*, 30, 401–9.

Silvestre, J. 1986: 'Undominated prices in the three good model'. *European Economic Review*, 32, 161–78.

Sneesens, H. 1984: 'Rationing macroeconomics: a graphical exposition'. *European Economic Review*, 26, 187–201.

Solow, M. and Stiglitz, J. E. 1968: 'Output, employment and wages in the short run'. *Quarterly Journal of Economics*, 82, 537–60.

Sondermann, D. 1985: 'Keynesian unemployment as non-Walrasian equilibria'. In G. R. Feiwel (ed.), *Issues in Contemporary Macroeconomics and Distribution*, London: Macmillan, 197–215.

Svensson, L. E. O. 1980: 'Effective demand and stochastic rationing'. *Review of Economic Studies*, 47, 339–56.

Svensson, L. E. O. 1985: 'Money and asset prices in a cash-in-advance economy'. *Journal of Political Economy*, 93, 919–44.

Tillmann, G. 1983: 'Stability in a simple pure consumption loan model'. *Journal of Economic Theory*, 30, 315–29.

Tillmann, G. 1985: 'Existence and stability of rational expectation-equilibria in a simple overlapping generation model'. *Journal of Economic Theory*, 36, 333–51.

Tobin, J. 1980: *Asset Accumulation and Economic Activity* (Yrjö Jahnsson Lectures). Oxford: Basil Blackwell.

Tobin, J. and Buiter, W. 1976: 'Longrun effects of fiscal and monetary policy on aggregate demand'. In J. Stein (ed.), *Monetarism*, Amsterdam: North Holland, 273–309.

Turnovsky, St. J. 1977: *Macroeconomic Analysis and Stabilization Policy*. Cambridge: Cambridge University Press.

Van den Heuvel, P. 1983: *The Stability of a Macroeconomic System with Quantity Constraints*. Berlin: Springer.

Varian, H. R. 1977a: 'Non-Walrasian equilibria'. *Econometrica*, 45, 573–90.

Varian, H. R. 1977b: 'The stability of a disequilibrium IS–LM model'. *Scandinavian Journal of Economics*, 79, 260–70.

Weinrich, G. 1982: 'On the theory of effective demand'. *Economic Journal*, 92, 174–5.

Weinrich, G. 1984a: *Effektive Nachfrage und Unterbeschäftigung bei stochastischer Rationierung, Europäische Hochschulschriften*. Frankfurt: Lang.

Weinrich, G. 1984b: 'On the size of disequilibrium in an equilibrium with quantity rationing'. CORE Discussion Paper No. 8418, Université Catholique de Louvain.

Weinrich, G. 1984c: 'On the theory of effective demand under stochastic rationing'. *Journal of Economic Theory*, 34, 95–115.

Weinrich, G. 1984d: 'On the structure of quantity rationing mechanisms'. CORE Discussion Paper No. 8429, Université Catholique de Louvain.

Weinrich, G. 1984e: 'A prototype macroeconomic model with stochastic quantity rationing'. CORE Discussion Paper No. 8417, Université Catholique de Louvain.

Weinrich, G. 1985: Price and wage dynamics in a simple macroeconomic model with stochastic rationing. Mimeograph, Florence.

Weitzman, M. L. 1985: 'The simple macroeconomics of profit sharing'. *American Economic Review*, 75, 937–53.

Younès, Y. 1970a: 'Sur une notion d'équilibre utilisable dans le cas où les agents économiques ne sont pas assurés de la compatibilité de leurs plans'. CEPREMAP, Paris.

Younès, Y. 1970b: 'Sur les notions d'équilibre et de déséquilibre utilisées dans les modèles décrivant l'évolution d'une économie capitaliste'. CEPREMAP, Paris.

Younès, Y. 1972: 'Intérêt et monnaie externe dans une économie d'échanges au comptant en équilibre Walrasien de court terme'. CEPREMAP, Paris.

Younès, Y. 1975: 'On the role of money in the process of exchange and the existence of a non-Walrasian equilibrium'. *Review of Economic Studies*, 42, 489–501.

Younès, Y. 1982: 'On equilibria with rationing'. In W. Hildenbrand (ed.), *Advances in Economic Theory*, Cambridge: Cambridge University Press, 147–73.

Index